D0190251

Thank You, Coach

"This book describes what the rapport between a coach and a player should be like and fully explores how each can achieve it. It paints a vivid picture of how each participant in that player/coach equation should respond at each opportunity that arises. And yes, it works for all employer/employee relationships as well."

— **Rick Page, Retired Texas High School Coach and Athletic Director**

"A wonderful thoughtful and inspiring read about what coaching and relationships are really about. A must read."

— **Dr. Fergus Connolly, Author of Game Changer -** *The Art of Sports Science*

"Winning Feels Incredible, Gratitude lasts a lifetime". Thank You Coach reveals Author Reid's success on and off the football field through lessons of a great coach. Within the pages of this book, athletes and business leaders will learn how to discover their greatness within through coaching.

– **Tom Dutta, CEO KRE-AT People Development, SUCCESS Coach to Executives, #1 International Best-Selling Author and Host of the** *Quiet Warrior Show*

"Football is more than a game. Step by step, blow by blow, Angus Reid pulls you into the games and onto the practice field of a professional football team as he relates how his coach for 11 years developed his skills and his outlook on life. Angus reveals the intricate details of how an exceptional coach helped him master techniques, control his emotions, deal with highs and lows, injury, and the end of his career. "Thank You Coach" is guaranteed to widen the perspective and tug at the emotions of anybody that has ever played, coached or watched the game of football."

– **Keith Johnston, author of** *The End Comes Quick: Lessons Live On*

"Thank You, Coach is a MUST-READ for every ATHLETE, COACH, STUDENT AND TEACHER. Angus identifies and elaborates upon one of the key aspects behind any successful person: the teacher-pupil relationship.

–   **Coach Nate Leonard, Duke University**

"I met both Angus and Dan this year for the first time. There is no doubt they had a great relationship. The lessons learned between player and coach can last a lifetime and 'Thank You Coach' is one of these lifetime lessons."

–   **Rick LeLacheur, President, B.C. Lions Football Club**

THANK YOU COACH

LEARNING
HOW TO LIVE
BY BEING TAUGHT
HOW TO PLAY

ANGUS REID

Copyright © 2018 by Angus Reid

All Rights Reserved. No part of this book may be used or reproduced in any manner whatsoever without written permission except in the case of brief quotations embodied in critical articles or reviews.

ISBN 978–1 9994165-0-8 paperback
ISBN 978-1-9994165-1-5 eBook

ABR Media
www.angusreid64.com

Cover Design: Blair Britstra Design
Interior Design and Layout: Priceless Digital Media
Back cover photo: Alan Wardle

To all coaches everywhere.
Thank you for giving your time
to better the lives of others.
You are my heroes.

ACKNOWLEDGEMENTS

Football is a game that is impossible to win alone. It takes an amazing team effort to even have a chance at success. I now know the same is true for writing a book. What I thought was going to be a solitary exercise proved to be a very similar undertaking as playing football. Writing a book is very much a team effort. And just like all my years playing ball, I have somehow found myself once again fortunate enough to be surrounded by such loving, giving, and talented teammates.

As with my football career, it would be impossible to mention each and every person that had a hand in my success. That would take more pages than all the books in the world combined. There are some though, who truly stand out – people who have continuously humbled me by their assistance with taking my crazy dream of writing a book and turning it into reality.

To my wife, Jennifer. Thank you for always indulging my crazy dreams and supporting me in my struggles to achieve them. Thank you also for being my sounding board for all aesthetic decisions needed for the project. You are my guiding light.

To my son, Brooks. Thank you for being my inspiration to keep going, even though many times I wanted to simply throw in the towel on this. You always make me want to be and do better.

To my parents. Thank you for always loving and believing in me. And thank you for being my early editors and always giving honest, constructive criticism of my work. You are the parents I strive to be.

To my four older brothers, Mark, Malcolm, John, and Bruce. Thank you for being great role models to look up to. I've just tried to be like you guys.

To my little sister, Mary. Thank you for always being my biggest fan. A brother couldn't ask for a better sister. You are the best.

ACKNOWLEDGEMENTS

To Keith Johnston. Thank you for all your early advice and guidance on all things needed to write and publish my own book. Your wisdom and introductions made much of this final product possible.

To my editor, Tracy Teel. Thank you for holding my hand through all of this and making my sometimes-rambling thoughts clear, concise, and meaningful. But mostly, thank you for giving me the belief that I can write. You have changed me.

To my book designer, Julie Price. Thank for dealing with all the headaches this rookie gave you. You are a true pro, and I have learned so much about this process from you. Next time will be smoother, I promise.

To my cover designer, Blair Britstra. Thank you for letting me talk you into doing your first book cover ever. I am blown away by how you took my vague vision and turned it into a masterpiece. You are a star!

To my good friend, Mark Smigel. Thank you for taking your own free time to help do final edits of my work. I am in awe of your generosity.

To my very first offensive line coach and first true mentor, Anthony Howie. I find it fitting that you gave my work the final review. I wouldn't have ended up where I am today if I hadn't started in your care so many years ago. Thank you for inspiring me to begin this football journey and helping me so much along the early part of that road.

To all the friends, coaches, and newly made acquaintances that encouraged me, supported me, and gave great feedback and advice every step along this journey. Thank you.

And finally, to Dan. Thank you for being the coach I needed, and in doing so, being the role model I have leaned on to guide me along the rest of my journey through this life.

I am eternally grateful.

CONTENTS

**"A GOOD COACH
CAN CHANGE A GAME.**

**A GREAT COACH
CAN CHANGE A LIFE."**

~ John Wooden

Photo by David Zuskind

With Coach Dan, helping me figure it all out.

PERSPECTIVE

A book which highlights the relationship between writer and subject often becomes a reflection of both. When a child, a student, an athlete, or an employee takes the time to express the deeply felt gratitude they feel for the mentoring and concern they have received, it must be accepted as momentous.

It is by no coincidence that Angus Reid and Dan Dorazio found one another.

Each man is of high character; each possesses the cherished qualities of loyalty, honesty, and integrity. Each is, in his own way, driven toward success.

I have had the privilege of being associated with both men for many years. Each remains emblazoned in my memory.

I first met Dan when he was a new hire of the Calgary Stampeders as our line coach. My first impressions of this man were that he was quiet, focused, determined. One who suffered fools lightly but with charity. He always appeared so busy that I would apologize to him whenever I interrupted his mission. I knew I couldn't talk football with him for fear he would quickly uncover how little I knew. I moved cautiously about him.

One day I happened to make a comment about going to church. His eyes lit up. It was as if I had revealed to him a secret that, in his mind, he thought I was okay. We talked about the Catholic Church and of the importance of our faith to each of us. This led to an interesting relationship between us. Dan, new to the league and to Canada, would scout out the locations and times of weekend services at Catholic Churches. This information he shared with me on those trips I was on. We began the habit of going to mass together when we were on the road. Dan's attendance at mass was inspiring. He prayed devotedly, listened to the preaching attentively, taking copious notes that he would read later. His enthusiasm for his faith was unbounded. From this, our relationship grew.

We had become comfortable with one another, so comfortable, in fact, that we began to talk football, family, and any topic of the moment.

Part of my responsibility was to observe coaches as they taught. The first moment I arrived at Dan's station at McMahon Stadium at the University of Calgary, I was in awe of him. His energy, stamina, enthusiasm, preparation, and true concern for his students made me feel this man had no peers. He was the bell measure by which other offensive line coaches were measured. He would, in addition to his charges, explain to me what he was doing and why in a manner so precise that even I understood it.

During games when we were on the sidelines together, we would talk. There was always tension on his face. I think he suffered more for the lineman who made a mistake during a game than the lineman felt for himself. Compassion was as natural an asset to Dan as was his ability to walk.

As time went on, Dan began to gain the respect of other Stampeder coaches. One morning before meetings I saw Chuck McMahon, one of our coaches, mopping his brow. He had just completed his first run with Dan. Chuck, whom I had known from our days in Montreal when he was a player and a former teammate of Wally Buono, blurted out, "We jog. Dan runs." That described Dan to a T. He was always in high gear.

I first heard Dan speak before a large group when he addressed a special teams meeting. His presentation was carefully thought out, articulately delivered, relevant and valuable. I added his public speaking abilities to his many talents.

Over the years, Dan and his wife Lisa and I became close friends. We visited one another when possible during the off-season. Lisa was ever mindful in sending me copies of newspaper articles in which I was mentioned.

The man I described is the man that Angus Reid is indebted to. If you know Angus, even slightly, he is the kind of person who is comfortable enough in his own skin to admit that a good part of his success is due to someone else.

Reid, by his own admission, had obstacles to overcome in order to achieve his goals. Recognizing these drawbacks and associating himself with someone like Dan who could and would help him work through them paved his road to success. They both journeyed through that road arm in arm in support of each other. Angus, the eager student; Dan, the insightful caring mentor.

Few, if any, marriages or relationships are made in heaven. This union was. It got off to a good start, picked up trust and intensity, and created an everlasting bond.

Angus had an important role in all of this. When Dan first reached out to him, Angus was receptive to the invitation. Instead of flaunting it and using it as a step up over his teammates, he respected it, took full advantage of it, and helped to solidify the bond that led to mutual success.

Angus with his gift of gregariousness and optimism amid a large portion of hope was a born leader. His teammates respected his grit, his determination, his never say die attitude.

The relationship between Dan and Angus shows me how two driven, determined people can climb a steep mountain while making it appear there is no slope.

More sports stories should reflect this bond. The relationships are there. In the words of Coach K of Duke University, "It isn't about winning and losing; it is about relationships."

– **Dr. Francis J. Lodato, Ph.D., ABPP, Psychological Consultant, BC Lions. Rct.**

Consulting Team Psychologist for 12 championship teams (NFL, CFL, NHL, NCAA)

VALIDATION

There is no way of saying everything I want to about Dan, or about this impeccably written testament of our coach by Angus. I will start with saying, that this is an absolute honour.

Dan came into my sporting life when I needed him the most. My last few years playing in the NFL, I found myself feeling jaded towards the sport that I loved for so many years. Dan's passion, desire, hard work, grit, and caring of individual's, the majority of which who were football players such as myself, was exactly what I was craving. He re-ignited the dwindling fire within me that allowed me to play for 7 years in the NFL and he helped me establish myself as the player that I was able to be within the CFL.

Throughout my career, I have been fortunate to play for some Hall of Fame coaches. I have the utmost respect and admiration for many of them, despite some challenging times. Dan was different. He made me feel like he was more concerned about me as a person, than as one of his players. He was not only a great coach, but to this day, continues to be a great man.

Moving to Canada to play in the CFL, with a number of years already playing in the NFL, there continued to be the running joke with my offensive linemen, that I didn't need coaching. Well, they were wrong, I did. At 29 years of age, I had many lessons to learn. Dan taught me to be a better team mate, a stronger leader, and a more efficient listener. In football, to be effective, we must have accountability to our fellow offensive linemen, dedication to our team mates, all while respecting the authority of our coaches. Those rules of engagement are a given. For me, the football code, was not only about football, but it was a code of living the life that I wanted to live, a life that I would be proud of. I think of Dan still to this day and adjust accordingly. Throughout my entire career in football, I never wanted to disappoint my teammates, but disappointing

Dan was not an option. Dan took me to the next level of playing the game by preparing us exhaustively for those 60 minutes of game day and building the necessary mental strength, days before that initial kick off.

Dan truly was someone who I would consider to be one of my Canadian father figures, and one that I was truly lucky to have. He was one of the most motivating people I had ever met and was a man that I not only had on my team, but always had by my side for my first three years in the CFL.

My first year in the CFL, I did the best I could to make Dan proud of me and to prove to myself and my team that I had earned the right to gain any accolades that I did. Being awarded the CFL Most Outstanding Lineman is one of my proudest moments; but, receiving a hug and a hand shake from Dan at the Player Awards Ceremony that night, continues to be one of my fondest memories. I continued to hold this feeling of pride, his motivating quotes and letters, words of wisdom and incredible encouragement throughout my time in Canada. Dan continues to influence me, and many of us, as is emulated in this book.

Dan, I have all of the letters you wrote to me as a BC Lion, and as a Toronto Argonaut. You truly emulate the best coaching I have received and I will ever be thankful for. Angus, thank you for writing this phenomenal testament of a man we both will always look up to, tell stories about, and respect. I love you both; a coach and a teammate that I will always be thankful for.

Anyone who reads this book will no doubt share my sentiments that Angus Reid is one of the best story tellers I have ever known and is a man of truths, honesty, and raw emotion. This book is for anyone who wants to better understand the impact of the coach/athlete relationship and wants to be inspired by the influence of a truly special coach.

- **Rob Murphy, 2 time Unanimous All – American (1997 – 98) The Ohio State University. Rose Bowl and Sugar Bowl Champion. 7-year N.F.L veteran. 6-year C.F.L veteran. 2006 Grey Cup Champion. 4-time C.F.L All-Star. 2-Time C.F.L Most Outstanding Lineman (2006, 2007)**

THE MYTH

Glinda: "The only person who might be able to help you would be the great and wonderful Wizard of Oz himself!"
Dorothy: "The Wizard of Oz? Is he good or is he wicked?"
Glinda: "Oh, very good, but very mysterious."
~ L. Frank Baum's *The Wizard of Oz*

A buddy of mine once told me a story about meeting Dan for the first time. It was 1998, and my friend Tony Martino was kicking for the Calgary Stampeders. Dan had just come on as their new offensive line coach. Tony walked into the team workout facility and saw this scrawny man climbing down off one of those original Stairmaster machines. He was completely drenched and had left a substantial pool of sweat on the ground below. Tony went over to introduce himself.

"Hi, I'm Tony Martino."

The man reached out and firmly shook Tony's hand. With an intense stare laced with a mischievous smile, one of which Tony says has never been matched, the man pointed with his other hand to the machine. Without breaking either the handshake or the eye contact, he responded, *"Tony, you see that Stairmaster over there? I just kicked its ass! Dan Dorazio. Great to meet you."* Not the kind of first impression a person tends to forget.

Tony went on and on about Dan – the man that never seemed to sleep yet always had more energy than anyone else. A man who would scream and yell all practice long but seemed to care more deeply about his players than any coach he'd ever seen. A man who sprinted everywhere he went as to not waste one more second of time than absolutely necessary yet was the most patient man he'd ever worked with. A ruthless taskmaster that demanded perfection of his players but who could always be seen with a smile on his face.

The stories were as bizarre as they were endless, but they were always comical. A part of me felt thankful that I didn't have a nut like that for a coach, but still, I was intrigued and fascinated by the extremes of how he balanced himself and his craft. What would it be like to have a coach like that? Soon enough, I would know firsthand.

THE BIGGEST ROOM IN THE WORLD IS THE ROOM FOR SELF-IMPROVEMENT.

INTRODUCTION

"Angus, can you hang around for a sec?"

It was Wednesday, October 3, 2013, and we had just wrapped up our day-three pre-practice meetings. There was a big game coming up that Friday against our long-time rivals the Saskatchewan Roughriders. We needed this win. We were 9–4 at the time and in a real dogfight in the west division heading into the home stretch of the season. This game mattered. The problem was: I didn't… not to the team anymore at least. You see, I hadn't played one down that entire season. I had been placed on the long-term injured list ever since the start of training camp when three badly herniated discs started crushing my sciatic nerve, rendering me pretty much immobile to nearly anything without excruciating pain. The hope was we could relieve the pressure with treatment and get through the season, but the issue just kept getting worse. By mid-September, all hope that I would be able to play again was gone. I was placed on the season-long deactivated list, and disc removal back surgery had been booked. After 13 seasons, multiple All-Stars, numerous years as a team captain, and two championships, I would finish my career as a glorified cheerleader. Truth is, I felt more like a ghost — there but not there; involved but not, part of the team but not part of it at all. So, when my coach asked me to stick around after meetings, I really had no idea what he could possibly want.

"Angus, I just wanted to let you know how much we really miss you out there. I…really miss you out there."

His words were sincere, and his facial expression conveyed nearly as much pain as I was feeling shooting down my left leg.

"I want you to know how bad I really feel for you."

The intensity of his eye contact, the clarity of his words, and his overall body language left no doubt that he meant it. In the 11 years I had known him, my coach had never minced words; each one was well thought out.

"I want you to know how very proud I am of you."

He was slow, deliberate, intense. Always intense.

"You've done everything I have ever asked of you to the very best of your abilities, every time. I couldn't have asked for anything more. I just want to make sure you know that."

I didn't know what to say. All I could embarrassingly muster was a very lame, *"Thanks, Coach."*

Dan Dorazio had been my offensive line coach for the last 11 seasons, a statement very few football players could ever make. In fact, the way my 13-year career started, he's pretty much the only pro position coach I ever truly had. He taught me everything I know about how to play football at this level. He had spent the last decade educating, training, testing, and evaluating not just my body, but my mind, spirit, and will. And now, it was all coming to an end.

This world I loved was ending. The real world was waiting on the other side. Football is a strange world. If you're not careful, the longer you stay in it, the more you may find yourself removed from knowing how daily life exists beyond training, practices, film study, game days, recovery, review, and repeat. It's a different life for sure. At that very moment, I finally realized that it really was over. I was never going to play football again. At age 37, I was going to have to learn an entirely new way of living. What skills did I have? All I ever did was everything my coach asked. Life was simple, not easy, but simple. I was coached and coached very well. Now, that would all be gone, and for the first time in my life I would have to know what to do all on my own. As I gingerly limped out of that meeting room, a jolt of terror washed over me. *"I'm screwed."*

"What the caterpillar calls the end of the world the master calls a butterfly"

~ Richard Bach

Unconsciously Learning How to Live

What I came to learn soon after my official retirement that winter was that I was going to be okay. What I did not realize at the time, and have come to see clearly now, was that even though Dan spent every single moment with me working to improve my ability to play the game, what he was really teaching me with every single moment was how to live. They say the greatest skills are those that transcend beyond the initial reason for teaching them. I call these transferable skills. To me, it's what sports are really all about – having an outlet to teach and learn valuable life skills that you can take with you after the sport is done and use in every other aspect of your life. The best coaches get this. They teach it through the sport. It's woven right within the meetings, drills, techniques, and competitions.

Dan is a true master of this. He teaches at such a level that you have no choice but to improve at the game, but in doing so you improve your ability to do almost everything else — that's true transferable skill coaching. In the end, that's what it's all about. What you can take with you when it's done. What you can use when it really matters — off the field, in the real game, your life.

So Much More than Just a Coach

I wish everybody could have had a coach like Dan. A mentor really. Somebody who can take you to levels of ability as an athlete and person that you never dreamed possible. Someone who lives what they teach, who cares more about helping people than they do about building their own résumé and ego. Someone whose greatest satisfaction is seeing his players do well on the field and in their life.

Whenever someone did something ridiculous during film or in practice, Dan used to joke, *"Someday, I'm going to write a book, and this will be in it."* If it was something really crazy, you might even be lucky enough to have Dan proclaim it would be getting its own chapter.

Well, I'm the one writing the book. And Dan is not only in it…the whole thing is about him. It's a thank you for everything he taught me as a player, but, more importantly, as a person. Knowing Dan, he would say he was only doing his job. But it wasn't his job that helped me…it's how he did it.

Nietzsche once said, "One repays a teacher badly if one remains only the pupil." From the moment I left that meeting room, I knew my days of being Dan's pupil were over. It was time for me to enter the next phase of my life. I didn't know it then, but Dan had armed me with everything I would ever need to be successful in whatever I chose next. That's how you repay your teacher – by taking what is taught and living it, wherever you are, whatever you may be doing. But for now, I need to simply say thank you.

Thank you, Coach.

WHEN THE STUDENT IS READY, THE MASTER APPEARS

My cell phone rang and showed BC Lions on the caller ID. My heart sank. It was mid-January 2003, and all I could think was they were calling to release me. You see, up to that point, my professional football career had been a series of let downs and disappointments. Two years earlier, I had been the Toronto Argonauts number one draft pick, taken fourth overall in the 2001 CFL draft. I was the top offensive linemen taken and the highest drafted Canadian school player. I remember that high, that feeling that I had made it, that all my dreams had now come true. After not having even started football until the 11th grade, then being severely sick and missing three of my five university seasons, I had proved that I belonged. That I had what it took.

The Argos quickly cut me following that first training camp. I had the distinct honor of becoming one of the very few, if any, number one draft picks that never even made it to the first week of practice with that club. I was a total and absolute bust. I basically begged my way onto the Montreal Alouettes' practice roster and was fortunate enough to dress for two games that initial season. Not that I saw any playing time — but it was nice validation to actually be in a uniform again on game day.

Week 15 of that first season, the Alouettes informed me that they were shipping me home to BC. They had struck a deal to gain the rights to Adriano Belli, a brutally powerful defensive lineman who the Lions had drafted but was not interested in playing for them. I took solace in the fact that I got a free flight home and that the Lions were willing to trade for me, even with the full knowledge that my trade value was for a player that was never going to play for them – ever. Good enough for me. I was heading to my hometown team. All was going to be right. Now my career could start.

I was regulated to the Lions' practice roster for the remaining three games of that first season. What a way to start a 13-year, 200 games played career. 3 teams, 0 downs played.

My second season didn't exactly begin any better. I had an old school position coach that played the bully role to force a response. I was struggling on the field and tanking between the ears. I was broken and actually believed the negativity that was being conveyed and immaturely packed it in. We hadn't even made it to the first exhibition game, and I had called it a career. I wasn't cut out for this. I guess I really didn't have what it took.

Thankfully, some distance and great guidance from my family and agent brought perspective and reality back to me quickly. You don't quit on your dreams no matter how much you're struggling and no matter what a coach is yelling at you every day. You fight. So, I returned. I made the club that year and dressed every game for my hometown team. Our Hall of Fame to-be center at the time, Jamie Taras, had a small injury, and I actually got to start two games. What a rush! Finally, out on the big field and playing for real. My first start went okay, probably because the team we were playing played an "even front," meaning they didn't put a player over me. It's not too hard to play decently when nobody is in front of you.

The second start – not so good. I ended up grading out at 46%. What does that mean? Well, a passing grade in a lineman's world is 90% or better. That means that 9 times out of 10 you did your job. I was only productive enough to do my job 4.6 plays out of every 10. That usually equals a very beat-up quarterback and a soon-to-be out of work lineman.

I survived that second season as a shaky backup center and an absolute imposter of a long snapper. A complete organizational shift after that '02 season led to a total coaching overhaul, but none of that changed the fact that I lacked confidence in my ability to perform at these levels and really had no proof to make me think otherwise. I was never going to quit again – but I really struggled to get myself to honestly believe I could make a career in this sport.

Then I answered that phone call. My career, and more importantly my life, would never be the same again.

Expect the Unexpected

"Angus…this is Coach Dan Dorazio calling."

I will never forget those words. They sounded so well thought out; they were said with such clarity and purpose. Not rushed, but not hesitant. It's hard to describe, but somehow I knew right there that this was a man that chose his words carefully and made sure every single one had real value and meaning. Nothing wasted — not even words. A no-nonsense kind of guy. Not arrogant or overbearing – just well thought out. This, I thought, was a man with a distinct purpose. I had only heard him say those six words and for some reason I felt a sense of overwhelming respect for him.

My New Coach

"Angus, I'd like to invite you to lunch…to get to know you bit. Very casual. Would YOU be okay with that? Is there a place near the facility YOU enjoy? When is a good time for YOU?"

It was strange. Everything was phrased in a way that put the power in my hands. Right away, I felt comfortable with this man. He had opened with a non-threatening invitation to lunch. It was phrased very specifically to emphasize that it was completely voluntary and totally up to me. Even the time and place were completely within my control. Up until now, I had never known choice in a player-coach relationship.

> **Assumption: Coach gives instructions;**
> **you do what you're told.**

That was pretty much it. I was never asked when, where, or how I would like things done before. Coaches never seemed that interested in my thoughts, mostly just my play.

Right from the start, Dan was different. His first contact was simply to arrange a voluntary football conversation; in fact, very little football was talked about at all. That led me to believe that he cared about me as an actual person. By explaining exactly what we were going to be doing, he lowered my anxiety and made me feel confident about what I was walking into. Because everything was phrased in question form, Dan made me feel important. My opinion, or at least my answers, mattered to him. Finally, by giving me some say in where and when we would meet for lunch, he removed the dictator assumption that many students enter a teacher/coach relationship with.

That simple phone call changed my entire mindset and overall outlook on my upcoming third pro season. Prior to that call, I'm not sure I honestly believed that I was going to make it in this league, let alone put together a 13-year career.

The Takeaway

Of all the amazing things a coach can do for an athlete, the most important is having the ability to put an athlete's mind at ease while eliminating all the other nonsense that stands in the way of their ability to completely focus on what really matters. Lower their anxiety early, and you will remove the obstacles that block them from buying into everything else you say and do – all those things that will really matter to their improvement.

COMMUNICATION – BUILDING TRUST

"People don't care how much you know until they know how much you care."

~ Dan

Boston Pizza. That's where I met Dan – my coach for the next 11 years – for the very first time. Not in our locker room, not in our meeting room, not in his office. Off-campus, casual, a non-football lunch. Just two people looking to get to know each other. Really, it was just Dan getting to know me. Lunch may have been an hour or so, and these are the six things I remember clearly:

1. **My initial reaction to his appearance.** Dan was not what you would physically expect when visualizing an offensive line coach. He was lean, wiry – oh, let's be serious…he's a rake! Maybe 5'10" with a slight hunch in his upper back that would get worse as practices or games wore on. He also dressed more professionally than I expected. Polished black loafers, tight-pressed slacks, and a neatly tucked in, crisp white 1984 Orange Bowl golf shirt with a collar so starched I thought there might be cardboard in it. (You did catch the date, didn't you? That shirt was nearly 20 years old!) Not exactly the body type or presentation one would normally expect for a guru for 300+ pound men. He was different, professional, serious, yet understated, and non-threating. He was perfect.

2. **The amount of pepper Dan put on both his soup and salad** that day may rival the amount of pepper that I have used in my entire life. It is something I have never witnessed before or since – truly legendary.

3. **His focus was on ME.** He always started an important question by saying my name. *"Angus, what non-athletic accomplishment are you most proud of?"* He would also pepper (no pun intended) my name throughout the conversation. This pattern continued my entire career. He did this with ALL of his players. Everything was personalized; he was always talking to YOU. You were always a person to him and who you were as that person was important.

4. **Most questions started with "what" not "why."** I didn't realize it at the time, but "what" questions are less threatening than "why" questions. He wanted to open the door for me to feel comfortable talking with him, not make me feel defensive. He always wanted to learn more about the other person. WHAT they were thinking was more important than WHY they thought it. One way leads to learning; the other leads to people always feeling interrogated.

5. **How well thought out and detailed his questions were.** They weren't stock questions, so I felt right away that he was sincerely interested in what he was trying to learn. He was prepared; he had given great thought to questions he wanted to ask. That theme became a hallmark of Dan's, and as proven by this conversation, not just in opponent prep, but in everything he did.

6. **His ability to listen.** Once his well thought out question was asked, all focus was on listening. He could stay quiet and let me talk FOREVER (which I am very good at). It wasn't about him; he never cared to hear himself talk. It was about listening to me. Learning about me. It was comforting knowing that what I said truly mattered to him.

The Foundation For What Lay Ahead

All the demands, criticisms, and failures that I would endure with Dan over the next decade were firmly placed in the context that this man truly cared about me and actually wanted to see me do well. My performance may have been "shitty" as Dan would far too often comment, but I always knew that he didn't believe I was. That separation is huge for an athlete to understand.

> **Assumption: Too frequently, athletes think,
> "The coach didn't like my performance;
> therefore, the coach doesn't like me."**

That can create an avalanche of negative emotions that disable the objectivity needed to simply work on correcting a technique. Dan removed that blurred way of thinking by beginning our relationship by caring about who I was as a person. He made it very clear that my worth as a person was in who I was, not in my ability to reach a defensive tackle on a wide zone. Those are two separate things and that must be made clear and reinforced frequently. It stops the negative self-talk and helps you remain objective. No need to protect a bruised ego. Just work on correcting the faulty technique.

I'm not saying I never took criticism personally or questioned what he thought of me. I'm only human and a very emotional one at that, but Dan continued to reinforce his belief in me and to express his gratitude to be able to work with me. That type of messaging goes a long way with athletes, especially when the majority of the 'work' chat is on pointing at your faults and highlighting areas that need improvement.

I always knew how much he cared about me, and that helped put everything else in perspective. Hard coaching, seemingly unreasonable demands, and constant performance-related criticism all came from a deep-rooted desire to see me succeed. It was the performance at any given moment that may have been unacceptable, not me. That was something I could always lean on. Even when I'd leave a film review thinking I must be the worst center in the world, I was still a valued person. The play just needed improving, and Dan would give me all he had to make sure we improved it. He wanted to see me succeed, and I believed it.

The Offer of a Jump Start

Lunch ended with an invitation to join him for some off-season workouts. This was 2003, and back then there were no guidelines or regulations on structured off-season training. Honestly, they simply didn't exist. The facility was open year-round, and many players were in daily to lift, run, do drills, or get treatment, but team organized activities just did not exist.

I jumped at the opportunity. By anyone's measure, I was an obsessive gym rat. I was always early to the gym, staying late, and doing extra workouts on the side. It was my life, and I loved every minute of it. And here was a coach who was willing to give me his time with one-on-one assistance to help prepare me as best as possible to perform as well as I could. A workout with my new coach was the least of my concerns. *"It'll be fun,"* I thought.

I Wasn't Ready for What Was Waiting

"Angus, how's 10 a.m. next Tuesday for you?"

Again, phrased to convey that I had some say.

"Works for me."

"I'll meet you in the locker room…10 a.m. sharp," he said, and that was that. We finished our lunch; he shook my hand, flashed a smile, thanked me for my time, and off we went. I couldn't wait for next Tuesday. What a perfect opportunity to make a great first impression with my new coach in the one area I knew I excelled.

<u>The Takeaway</u>

In hindsight, he REALLY wanted to get to know me. Who I was and what made me tick. What values and interests I pursued. I realized, much later, what Dan had long known: in order to really care about others, you need to really know them, and that means spending quality time with them, asking important questions, and actually listening and caring about their answers – there is no way around that.

WHAT I GAVE DAN
TO WORK WITH

"Angus, your feet are half the size, so they're going to have to move twice as fast."

~ **Dan**

There's an absolutely hilarious radio clip on YouTube from the morning of the 2006 Canadian Football League annual player draft. The Lions had just selected Dean Valli, a promising young offensive lineman from my old alma mater, Simon Fraser University. I didn't know it at the time, but that selection was a strategic pick to choose and groom my replacement. Why? Because they wanted someone bigger, someone who looked the part more than I ever could. The station had Dan on discussing the Lions' pick, talking about who Dean was, and why the Lions drafted him in the first round.

Typed words cannot do it justice, but here is Dan's response to what you want when **looking** at an offensive lineman. In particular, what Dan saw in Dean:

*"He's 6'5" measured, that's true, and he's 305. Those measurements right there…he's got good girth. He's got a good-looking body. He's got a body…**he's got a real body**. No flab on him. He's a real good-looking guy. **It's what you want. He's what you want.**"*

Look it up. Trust me. You won't regret it. It's gold. Pure gold. And it's pretty much bang on, too. There is a certain body type that football wants from their offensive lineman. A body like Dean's is what offensive line coaches want. A body like mine? Not so much.

Football, as you can imagine, is a sport generally reserved for the biggest, strongest athletes in the world, particularly when you're talking about offensive lineman — the position I played. We're the five big guys up front whose job it is to basically push people out of the way for a living. My day-to-day activities at work revolved around two basic premises. On a running play, find a way to drive another 300 lb. man out of the way, so he can't tackle the guy carrying the ball. On a passing play, stop that same 300 lb. man from getting by you (or running over you), so your quarterback doesn't get blasted and is able to throw the ball. Simple really, just not easy. Kind of like life.

With thousands upon thousands of applications each year, pro football has no shortage of willing players wanting an opportunity to play the sport they love at the highest level. With that type of willing workforce, pro football has the luxury of being very specific about what they're looking for from would-be players. There are so many traits that make up a good offensive lineman physically, mentally, and emotionally, that it would be impossible to have a simple résumé criterion for teams to make their hiring decisions. Players need to be evaluated, interviewed, and tested on an individual basis before final picks get made. Even then, the process is far from an exact science, but the vetting process must start somewhere. That somewhere usually begins physically. Given the basic job description, there are four specific body characteristics that will give a potential lineman a physical advantage over others. These traits are heavily coveted by scouts, coaches, and teams as they are characteristics that cannot be created or improved on. You either have them, or you don't.

#1 – Height

> **Big people move smaller people easier
> than smaller people move big people.**

Because of that reality, generally speaking, offensive lineman are the largest athletes in the world, routinely weighing in at over 300 lbs. (some are even over 350 lbs.) Now, bear in mind that many of these men can dunk a basketball and probably move faster over short distances than most humans half their size. These are true athletes. To carry that much weight in a manner that allows such athleticism requires a large surface area. The longer the body, the easier it is to carry more weight and still be productive. Today, professional offensive lineman average somewhere between 6'4" and 6'6," with the outliers being 6'7" – 6'8" on the tall end, and 6'3" MAYBE 6'2" on the short end. Being too tall makes it difficult to get low enough to gain any leverage on the person you're trying to move. Too short and there's not enough body surface to carry enough weight required to move another large human.

Me: I'm 5'13". Seriously, I'm so barely 6'1" that I was known my entire career as the "little one." Sounds crazy when you weigh in at 300 lbs., but that is how big these men are. You learn quickly that everything in life is relative. Where 6'1" 300 lbs. is huge in 99% of circumstances, I'd find myself too short when viewed through the eyes of a professional football team choosing their linemen.

#2 – Wingspan or Arm Length

> **When blocking another man attempting to either drive him out of the way or shielding him from getting around you – he who makes contact first usually wins.**

This is simple. If I can get my hands on you before you can get yours on me, I have the advantage. Quickness helps for sure, but if I can physically reach you from a distance, I have a mechanical advantage that if coached well cannot be defeated no matter how much you bench press. After all, what good is strength if you can't even reach the other person to use it?

The longer the arms, the greater the advantage. Long bodies usually come with long arms. A proportioned athlete's wingspan often matches his overall body length. If you're 72" tall, your wingspan will probably be the same. Once again, longer bodies help here, too. There are always outliers here as well, and this is where some shorter linemen can make up the difference.

Sometimes you're lucky enough to find athletes with exceptionally long arms in proportion to their height. A true prize for sure. I'd bet that most offensive linemen in professional football that are 6'3" or under have a wingspan greater than their body length. That slight tweak in proportions helps make up what they lack in height. In fact, some athletes have wingspans that are four, five, even six inches longer than their height!

My wingspan: 4"— 4" **shorter** than my height, that is. Not only was I too short, but my arms were disproportionately shorter. Bottom line: I'm built like a turtle, and turtles don't play the offensive line professionally – giants do.

#3 – Hand Size

> **The bigger the hand, the stronger**
> **it either is or can be made to be.**

All offensive linemen grab. No, it's not holding; it's blocking. It's controlling the defender and then driving him somewhere of your choosing. Do this right now, open your hands and spread your fingers apart as wide as possible. Measure the distance from the outside edge of your pinkly to the outside edge of your thumb. What number did you get? If it's less than nine inches across, you have small hands by pro football offensive lineman standards. I've played with guys that have hands that are over 10 inches across. Some are around 11 inches! You know what guys with size 10 and bigger hands can do to you? Anything they want!

Big hands = strong grip = more control over the person you are trying to control or move. You can't make your hands bigger; they're either big enough or they aren't. Mine: not quite an eight. STRIKE THREE.

#4 – Foot Size

> **The greater the surface area contacting the ground,**
> **the more force you can generate and the greater**
> **stability you will have once contact is made.**

Almost all the offensive linemen I played with over my 13-year-career had shoe sizes of 14 and up. 15 was probably the overall average. I even played with a guy who wore a size 19! Good luck pushing him over. Forget how big he was; he had snow shoes for feet! That's stability; that's also power. Your feet are what connect you to the almighty ground. The greater that connection is, the more functional you can be.

My shoe size: 11 ½. 0 for 4. I didn't even come close to meeting any of the basic physical requirements to be considered for that career. I did NOT have a good-looking body, not by football standards anyway. Mine was NOT a body offensive line coaches would love to look at. I'm not what you want. I'm not what Dan wanted. I am what he had, though. I was the young center he inherited when he came on board to coach. I was what he had to work with. He would tease me from time to time about my size (or lack thereof), but I knew it was always strategically placed whenever he felt I could use a little extra juice in my blood.

<u>The Takeaway</u>

Dan knew when to poke and when to praise. That came from taking great care in learning who we were and what made us tick. Never once did I hear Dan complain about having to work with me. Coaches get judged on the performance of their players. It's only natural to want the very best raw material with which to work – **but you don't complain about the hand you're dealt. You focus on playing the cards you've got as well as you possible can.**

Dan dealt with the reality he had at that time. He gave me everything he had and pulled every ounce of ability he could out of my undersized, awkwardly built, stumpy, fire hydrant body. I was at a physical disadvantage for sure. There was only one way for me to make up the difference, and Dan knew what that was – work! So, that's exactly what we did.

TRAINING – LEAPING PAST LIMITS

"If you want to leave footprints in the sands of time, wear work boots."

~ Dan

Tuesday 9:30 a.m. I was dressed in my workout gear, sitting at my locker stall, ready to go. Being early is a trait that was programmed into me by my mother from a very young age. "Better to be an hour early than a minute late" was the mantra repeated in our house again and again. It's been drilled into my DNA, and I realize there are far worse traits to have (I have many of those, too), so, I waited.

At exactly 9:59 a.m. Coach Dorazio came through the doors. He was wearing beat-up team-issued sweatpants and a team-issued hoodie that had to be three sizes too big. Two questions instantly popped into my head:

1. If he'd just started coaching here, why was his team gear so old?

2. Why couldn't we get him some clothes that fit?

I never bothered asking those questions because I quickly found out that he wasn't trying to impress me with his outfit. He was there to get work done, nothing else.

The other thing that stood out was the large wooden box sitting directly in the middle of the locker room. I had never seen it before, but it was roughly three feet high and close to being square. It had some textured tape strips on the top and had obviously been custom made. I was pretty sure it was a box used for plyometric jumping. But where did it come from, and why was it sitting in the middle of the locker room? I should have known.

At exactly 10 a.m., not a second earlier, Dan flashed a grin and asked, "Ready to go?" This time he wasn't looking for my answer. It was time to get to work.

There was no warm up. When I say we didn't warm up, I don't mean we eased into the workout at some slow gradual tempo. Nonsense! We went right to it. That big box that seemed so out of place minutes earlier immediately became my new nemesis.

Jump to It

Dan had me stand with the 36" high box just to my right.

"I want you to jump on this box and twist your hips to the right, so when you land on the top, you will be facing completely the opposite way."

No sweat. He wanted me to do a plyometric box jump. I had done these for years. The box height was not too high for me, even at 310 lbs. I had built great lower body explosiveness from years of squatting and Olympic weight lifting, but I had never been asked to start at a box's side and do a 180 up. But really…how hard could it be?

"Once you're on the top," his eyes were piercing through me now, *"I want you to step off the other side and immediately upon touching the ground do a 180 back up, so you're once again facing the other side."*

Okay…this was starting to sound a bit harder now. Dan heightened his stare.

"Get your hips ALL the way around, and don't waste time on the ground, that was now an order. *We're going to build your hip explosiveness, flexibility, and endurance all right here."*

Still, I wasn't too worried…until I heard the rep/set scheme.

"We'll do four sets of 10 jumps with 30 seconds rest between."

I'm sure I saw a smile in his intense stare, like he knew damn well what was going to happen to me and took some sort of strange pleasure in that knowledge. The first few jumps were easy. I had more than enough power to get my stout 310 lb. body up on that box. I was rebounding off the ground so fast that a sense of immense pride came over me for just the slightest moment. *"I must be impressing him,"* I thought.

"Get your damn hips around!" Dan barked.

Apparently, my initial assessment didn't equate to his.

"Move faster and get those damn hips around more!"

I thought I was. Okay. More hip spin, faster rebound off the ground, push harder, dig deeper. I can do this. I finished the first set with two new realities:

1. I don't move as fast as I think I do (who really does?).

2. My hips are not nearly as flexible as I thought they were (whose really are?).

Well-programmed drills isolate and expose inherent weaknesses that force you to face reality and avoid compensation tactics. You strengthen that weakness through consistent repetitions in that exposed environment, allowing for adaption and improvement in that specific area. As Dan gave me the 3-second countdown to the start of set two, I was already clearly aware of two glaring gaps in my physical state: my hips were too tight, and my endurance was nowhere near what it needed to be.

"3, 2, 1 – GO!"

It was like the start of an Indy race. Dan would not allow a second to go to waste, not even during the transfer of rest back to work.

"Move! Move! Move!" he barked.

By the fifth rep of the second set, the lactic acid was building. Thirty seconds was not enough rest for my body, at least not enough based on its prior knowledge of adequate rest. That was the reality my body HAD known; this was the new reality it now had to deal with and face.

The quality of my jumps was deteriorating quickly. By the end of my second set, I had already made up my mind that I would not be able to finish a third. No way. I told Dan I needed a longer rest. Without hesitation, he barked back, *"Bullshit to that!"* In his 11 years as my coach, it was the only cursing I ever heard him say. It was less said to me and more a battle cry laughing back at the gods of fear and uncertainty.

"You can do this, now let's go!"

Without any other comment on the subject, he jumped right back to the phrase that became all too familiar with those workouts, *"3,2,1 – GO!"* Like Pavlov's dog, I responded and leapt on the box. Dan's orders removed time for thinking and charged me to action. The reps seemed to grow higher, and the rest seemed to get shorter. They didn't, obviously, but that's how distorted your view of reality can become when you're pushed to the limit. It felt as though I had a boa constrictor around my chest and 300-pound weights on my legs.

Coach wouldn't let me stop. He didn't allow me to indulge in the pain, rest a little longer, or do a few less reps. No. The only way through this was THROUGH IT. You do what is expected and demanded and needed of you in whatever situation you find yourself in, always. All these years later, I'm still very proud of the fact that I finished all 40 reps that first workout. They weren't pretty, and I doubt in the end they transferred much technical benefit to my on-field performance. I also finished everything else from that first torture test of a workout as well. We did these never ending wall punching drills. The same concept as the box jumps, only now we were building my explosive punching endurance. The reps were crazy high, and the rest was ridiculously short. My arms were complete jelly, but Dan would never allow me to give in to the pain or the distraction that was baiting me to quit. He showed me that I could keep going, even if I didn't believe that myself. He just kept screaming technique cues and words of encouragement. The cues were important; they kept restoring my focus. Those 90 minutes seemed to never end. Every time I felt myself wanting to slow down or give in to the exhaustion and the very real lactic acid and lack of oxygen, I could hear Dan's voice in the back of my head, saying, *"Bullshit to that! You can do this, now let's go!"* So, I kept going.

The Takeaway

What I learned that morning was something much more powerful than the need for explosive endurance and functional hip mobility. I learned how much more I always have in the tank, and that choosing to quit or keep going are decisions that are always completely within my control.

CHOOSING AN IRON WILL

"Between stimulus and response, there is a space. In that space is our power to choose our response. In our response lies our growth and our freedom."

~ Victor Frankl

Life is always about choice. We choose to move forward or not. We choose to keep going or decide that we can't. It's all a matter of perspective, and that perspective can be greatly influenced by our level of training and our degree of conditioning. Vince Lombardi once famously said, *"Fatigue makes cowards of us all."* Fatigue shoves its face in front of your ambitions and goals and gives you the out. It presents a (seemingly) real obstacle that helps us justify quitting.

Most people allow fatigue to dictate their ability to continue. They have (consciously or unconsciously) empowered an outside source to decide their limits. Dan taught me the power of reclaiming that decision for myself. Victor Frankl talks about a space, however brief, between stimulus and response, between feeling the exhaustion and actually stopping. Building a wedge means reclaiming that space and consciously choosing for ourselves whether or not to continue — never relinquishing that control to anything or anyone outside of yourself. This may be one of the most powerful skills one can build.

Limits Are Mostly a Matter of Choice

It can be incredibly hard to build this alone. Great coaches push their athletes not just to improve their ability to perform a physical skill on the field, but to improve their ability to know that they can always do more, more than they ever thought possible. It's not a coach's job to simply find a player's breaking point. That takes no skill and has no value beyond taking athletes to failure, what good is that? **Great coaches help their players past their perceived breaking point.** They push and pull them through to the other side. Sure, that usually means getting even more out of them on the field of play, but really, they have shown them that they can always do more than they thought.

Remember Those Box Jumps?

We did those box jumps every single workout, sometimes multiple days in a row. I slowly got better at them. My body adapted and improved. Dan kept changing the reps and sets. Sometimes eight sets of five; sometimes five sets of eight. Once, we did one set of 40. That was straight up crazy, but I got them all. The only one harder than that was doing two sets of 20. Maybe that sounds easier, but it's not. Two things make it harder because:

1. Physically, you give the lactic acid time to rush in and fill your legs during that 30-second rest period, which creates the illusion that they have each just gained 300 pounds of dead weight.

2. Psychologically, you give your body the chance to realize how tired it is and give your brain the time to process how crazy it is to keep going.

That's where the wedge gets built — having every reason physically and mentally to stop but making the decision to keep going anyway. You build the wedge by maintaining the role of decision-maker, regardless of all the crap that's happening to your body and going through your mind. You stay focused on the mission, consciously acting out of choice, not just reacting as a physical response.

Box jumps were just one of the countless torture tests Dan put me through. The list is long and diverse. From the usual suspects, like pushing his car up the road and endless split squat jumps, to things a little more exotic and drastically cruel. The endless broad jumps onto my face while harnessed to a hundred or more pounds, to the dreaded step, step, touch drill, while swinging around three quarter full kegs (of water, I presumed). Most, I would never have done willingly, nor believed were even humanly possible. Yet, in all my years, I never missed a rep. I never once failed to complete any drill we started.

> **The ability to keep going, to finish what you started, is not a gift; it's just a choice.**

Dan built my wedge initially by not giving me a choice. He wouldn't allow me to stop. He knew what was possible even if I didn't. He made sure I didn't quit on myself early on, and, in doing so, showed me I didn't have to. I could always do more; he just had to pull me through my disbelief. He constantly pushed and pulled me to exertion levels I would have never come close to accomplishing on my own. I wouldn't have had the ability to drive myself to those extremes — but in getting me there, I built the knowledge that I could, which gave me the strength to choose to keep going when, previously, all physical signs would have overwhelmed me into quitting.

Mid-way through my career, complaints from players on the extreme nature of Dan's workouts created enough noise for the team to instruct Dan to 'water them down.' I'll never forget his response to my inquiry on why we were easing up. It was less of an answer and more of a statement — a statement on his global view of the current times, and a personal warning and plea to me:

"The whole world's going soft. Don't let it make you soft, too."

Soon after that, the league itself rolled out more formalized rules for what a coach could do with a player directly in the off-season as it related to physically training them. I understand the reasoning; I also saw the ramifications. Football and life aren't going to water down their demands on you just because you watered down your preparation. Your training needs to be at a level that matches the demands you will face. Otherwise, quality under real pressure will diminish.

> **You don't rise to the level of your expectations; you fall to the level of your training.**

The Value of Building My Wedge

I had been lucky for sure. I avoided the devastating injuries that sideline so many players, but the daily grind and abuse on the body would have given me many opportunities to cash in a day off here or there or maybe a lightened load from time to time. *"Bullshit to that!"* came to mind whenever my thoughts would drift toward stopping, easing up, or feeling sorry for myself. Life isn't about how we can get out of doing things, but how we can keep doing what we choose to do better, no matter what the situation. That's all a choice — one we get to make again and again and again.

By Fall 2009, I had played in an incredible 142 consecutive games, starting each and every one of them. Maybe more impressive than that was the fact that I had never even missed a single practice in that 7-year stretch. That was until October 24, 2009 on a cold late autumn day in Regina.

We were in a classic slugfest with our long-time rival the Saskatchewan Roughriders. Playing in Regina had always been the most difficult, yet rewarding road trip destination in my entire career. They have the most loyal, energetic, and flat out loud fan base in the entire league. Playing them meant having two opponents: the team and the crowd.

It was mid-third quarter, and we ran a wide zone running play to the right. A true bread and butter play for our offense. I had run this play a thousand times and could do it in my sleep. After snapping the ball, I sprinted to my right and looked to shove any defender in that area out laterally to create a space for the running back to turn up. I would continue up the field, sprinting on a diagonal, looking for any flowing linebacker that I could lock up with and keep from tackling our runner.

All was going smoothly. I had successfully climbed to the second level and engaged perfectly with a smaller flowing linebacker — then it happened. I felt an avalanche hit my back. A second linebacker had snuck in from behind and catapulted himself into our running back, who was wisely tucked in behind my escort block. As the two men crashed into my back, my right toe got spiked directly into the hard (older style) field turf. The crack was immediate. Before I even hit the ground, I knew what I had done. My foot was broken. More precisely, it was broken in half. I learned later I suffered what is called a Lisfranc fracture. I had shattered the bones across the top of my foot and torn the ligaments that held those bones together. The only things holding my foot intact were my skin and my shoe. Not the best situation to find yourself in. Of course, I didn't know the severity of it all right then. What I did know was that I had never felt acute pain like that before, and I was quite certain that I couldn't walk.

"Bullshit to That"

As I lay there on the turf, our medical staff came rushing out. The pain was overwhelming and baiting me to give it all of my attention, to empower it to make the decision for me. Then, deep in the back of my mind, the wedge that Dan had spent so many years building in me shouted, *"Bullshit to that! You're always in charge of your decisions, always. For good or bad. Fatigue, pain, whatever can never be given the power to make a coward out of you. A strong wedge gives you the power to decide."*

I decided I was going to keep playing. Right or wrong, I was in charge of what I was going to do. How was I going to do it? I had no idea, just as I had no idea how I would ever finish that first workout of box jumps. That "how" can always be worked out, though. It's choosing that you will do something that matters.

I told them I had badly rolled my ankle, but I doubt they bought it. As they helped me to the sidelines for closer examination, it became clear that I couldn't walk. This was real pain now. The few minutes of examination had allowed my foot to swell and expand to the limits that both my skin and probably more realistically my tightly wrapped up shoe would allow.

"Give Me a Couple of Aspirin."

I had a ton of credibility, and who would lie about something like this anyway? I was adamant about keeping that shoe on. Taking it off would've been game over for sure. The evidence would have been obvious, plus there would have been no way in hell to get my ever-expanding foot back into that shoe even if they would have let me.

They bought my bluff. They wrapped my shoe as tight as possible with a second layer of tape. That alone was more pain than I care to voluntarily endure again. I assured them that I would be fine and that we could deal with the sprain after the game…then I assembled my fellow linemen and told them the truth.

"Guys, I can't walk," which I immediately followed up with, *"so here's what we're going to do."* I wish I could remember the look on their faces as I outlined my plan to keep going. Sherko and Dean played directly to the right and left of me, and my plan was for them to help me from the huddle to the line of scrimmage for each play. *"Huh?"* was their non-verbal facial response. "Sherk, I'll put my right arm on your shoulder; Dean, I'll put my left arm on yours, and I'll hop up to the line on my left foot." It sounded like a good plan to me; no way I would've gotten away with that, though. Could you imagine the look on the d-lineman's face if my guards had basically carried me up the line of scrimmage? *"On second thought, I'll get to the line myself. No worries. It might just take a few more seconds than normal."* They thought I was crazy and looking back I would tend to agree with them. It's fascinating, though, how you can deal with any issue no matter how painful if you've learned to stay focused on the mission without letting outside issues distract you from getting your work done. To continue or not, rightly or wrongly, is always YOUR decision. So, I continued.

Our defense held them to a quick 2 and out, and we were ready to take the field again. This all happened so fast that Dan hadn't had time to check on me yet. As I began my march back on the field with the rest of the offensive, Dan yelled over to me in disbelief, *"You're finished for the day, right?"* I looked back at him with the best Dan scowl I could muster and barked, "BULLSHIT TO THAT," and off I went to finish the mission.

I battled through the rest of that game. The pain was excruciating, and my performance I'm sure dictated that. But for each 3–5-second play interval, I was able to switch all focus to the task. With each play, I made the decision to keep playing, never allowing my shattered foot to decide for me.

To add insult to injury, the game went to double overtime! What were the odds? We were also forced in a few situations into a no-huddle, hurry up offense. I can honestly say that day tested the absolute limits of my wedge. I will also say that by no means would I ever encourage anyone to play on a shattered foot. Looking back, it was not a smart thing to do. The point is that I retained the right to make the decision. I didn't let pain dictate what I was going to do.

The Takeaway

We don't have to be reactionary animals. We choose our life moment to moment. For good or for bad, it's always up to you. Dan's constant pushing of my physical limits enabled me to see how much more I always had and that doing more was simply a choice. That may be the most empowering feeling of all. Having an iron will is nothing more than choosing one. It takes a great coach to get a player to not only understand that but to also believe it to the point that they come to the realization that they're only really done when they choose to be. Quitting for any other reason? *"Bullshit to that!"*

ON ALWAYS BEING READY TO GO

"You ever see a cheetah warm up?"

~ **Dan**

That first workout, and every single one after it, started with a "You ready to go?" from Dan, and then we just went. It wasn't really a question so much as a statement. No stretching, no 'functional' warmup, no easing in. We just went. 0–100, like that. I thought he was completely crazy, but when you remove the ability to warmup, you stop needing to. In keeping with Dan's fanatical maximization of time, he saw warming up as purely a waste of it. You're either working, or you aren't. There was no getting ready to work.

It brought me back to my childhood. As kids we never warmed up to play; we just played, 100 mph right from the word "recess." I realize as we get older and more beat-up, particularly as athletes, there is a tendency to always be tight. Trust me, I'm no different. My extremely short and very thick legs gave me hip flexors that were knotted like softballs and hamstrings that felt like guitar strings. I was always tight. Dan's response to my very first inquiry regarding warmups gave me the key to being able to always go.

"You ever see a cheetah warm up?"

My first response was going to be, "No, but what about a rhino?" Thankfully, I thought better to keep my mouth shut until I knew this man a little longer. Turns out, he was right about the cheetah; it doesn't warm up. In fact, humans are the only creatures that need to warm up. Every other animal just goes when it's time to go. They also don't sit in chairs all day, and they stretch periodically throughout the day, always staying limber and always keeping their bodies ready to go at a moment's notice.

Always Be Ready to Go

That's where I found my answer. I couldn't avoid sitting in chairs, but I could stretch throughout the day whenever a moment or two allowed. Nothing drastic, though, just some simple mobility drills I had picked up over the years, enough to never allow my body too much time in between athletic exertions to get too tight. I just did what was needed to make sure my body was always ready to go.

What it really came down to was a shift in mindset. Along with saving time, Dan was always looking to remove any crutch that you may have felt you needed in order to do your job. Becoming so psychologically reliant on an elaborate warmup routine puts you at a huge disadvantage if a situation comes about where that isn't an option. You better be able to simply 'go.'

Wait, Wait, Go!

I started my 10th professional season as a backup. The shattering of my foot the season prior had left me with two large surgically implanted crisscrossed screws holding my foot in place. The screws did not allow for any foot flexion, thus giving me, in essence, a solid brick for a right foot. The club decided that I would no longer be able to perform at a starter's level. They'd also given me the option to play my 10th season as a backup. The expectation was for me to mentor my successor, maintain a locker room leadership role, and act as an insurance policy, if needed, then to retire to much fanfare at season's end. I publicly accepted the demotion. Privately, though, I vowed to regain my spot to once again lead the line from on the field. I did all I could to fulfill my obligation to mentor, lead, and keep myself ready to go both mentally and physically.

Then it happened. Fate, luck, whatever you want to call it. I find once your mind is set so clearly on what you want, life always throws you at least a sliver of opportunity. The question is, will you be ready to go, or will you have to ask that opportunity to wait a few minutes while you warm up?

Mid-second quarter of game three that 2010 season, I was one of two backups with the very clear understanding that I was the 7th man (the backup to the backup), and the team's very last choice to have to put in and play. This belief was reinforced as our right guard suddenly went down with a badly rolled ankle. Unable to continue, I saw our head coach Wally Buono look down the sidelines. It was me and our rookie draft pick from that year. They put the rookie in. I knew right then they had no intention of ever having me play again.

A Second Second Chance

Only a few short plays later, though, their hand was forced. One of our other guys went down. Wally now had no other option than to put me in. I couldn't believe it! I was getting my chance to prove that I still belonged out there on the field. Time to shine again. My first few seconds were those of pure shock, and the next moments were spent scrambling to try and find my helmet! I had been so sure I would never be getting in that it wrongly wasn't in my hands ready to go. By the time I threw my lid on, it was time to get out there and call the huddle. As I began my short sprint from the sideline to the field, Dan grabbed my shoulder pad and, with his usual intense stare, asked me the same question he had asked so many times before: *"You ready to go?"* I knew he already knew the answer. I just smiled, winked, and confidently responded: *"What do you think?"*

I was 34-years-old with an immobile and already completely arthritic foot. I suppose warming up would have been nice, but life doesn't always give you that option, so you better not rely on getting it. Two deep squat jumps in the huddle and off we went...just like old times. The play got called; we marched up to the line; I barked out the blocking scheme, snapped the ball, and unleashed hell.

0–100, Just Like That

I played that game as if it was the last I would ever play. I honestly thought it would be. Players would recover, and I would be returned to the bench. Funny thing...I ended up playing one of the finest games of my career. A near perfect 97% grade. Plenty of knockdowns and downfield blocks to boot. I played with the energy and excitement of a teenager... all without a moment of traditional warm up.

I performed well enough to eventually win my starting job back, playing another three seasons, earning two more All-Star selections, and winning another Grey Cup.

The Takeaway

Now, I'm not against warming up one bit, and I doubt Dan is either. I've just learned not to rely on it. Dan trained me to be prepared to go at a moment's notice. Years of training had removed that mental need for preparation. I no longer needed it before taking action. Always be ready because life won't necessarily give you warning or time to warm up. When the bell tolls, you better be ready to go.

LEARNING HOW TO LEARN – PART 1

THE POWER OF VISION

"If you can't see yourself win the block, then you probably won't."

~ Dan

"Pronate!...PROOOONNNNATE!...HOLD...HOOOOOLD... BREAK!"

Dan slapped my tensed glutes on the word "BREAK!" I could relax now. My feet had hardly moved in the last 10 minutes, yet my whole body was already feeling the fatigue. It was my first introduction to the Ray Crowther blocking sled. Actually, I had seen the thing sitting on our practice field ever since Dan arrived in town. I found out later, having this sled was one of his only absolute equipment demands. He loved this sled. The Crowther has been around since 1932 and has really enjoyed a strong comeback in the modern coaching world. In 2003, though, it was seen as an antique, an oddity, the way things USED to be done. Not for Dan. It was a necessity. I was now learning why.

Learning in the Dark

We had actually started this training day about 45 minutes earlier in Dan's office. It was the first time we had done any film work together. I wasn't sure what was on the agenda, but I was excited to find out. It was also the first time I had ever been in Dan's office. What a sight! Dan had two entire walls of VHS tapes. I'd never seen a football video library like that before or since. What was even more impressive was the thought-out groupings and meticulous arrangement of the tapes themselves. He gave the Dewey Decimal System a solid run for its money. Dan had tape categories for anything and everything an offensive line coach could ever imagine wanting. He even had a section with a tape dedicated to every single meaningful defensive lineman in our league. I'm serious! An individual tape for each player. Tapes filled with all the most dangerous moves and predictable tendencies they had shown in any game they had played as a pro. Have an offensive line question? Dan has a tape with the answer. I'd put Dan's film database up against Google any day.

Videos and a large screen to watch them on. Lights off. All focus on the film. He'd often proudly wear his C.O.O.L. T-shirt. It's a club for offensive line coaches that meet yearly to share strategies, best practices, etc. C.O.O.L stands for Coaches of Offensive Lineman. The logo on the shirt was a big cartoon mushroom, kind of like the one in the Smurf cartoons. When asked why they would pick a mushroom for their logo, Dan's response was always instant and always the same – *"Because offensive line coaches eat shit and live in the dark."* He always seemed to enjoy giving that response. I can't comment on the "eat shit" part, but I can confidently say Dan lived most of his working life in the dark. He might have meant that figuratively, but I saw it literally. His office was always pitch black except for the light from the film. That's what mattered because that's where the information was. And for that first meeting at least, that's where my learning how to learn began.

The "tape" as Dan still calls it "rolled." We watched 45 minutes of Jamie Crysdale executing perfect form on the Crowther sled. Jamie was Dan's long-time center in Calgary where he had been coaching the previous five seasons. Jamie was a natural technician, but this film was obviously the visual result of many hours working with Dan on this specific technique. It was perfection in motion. We watched clip after clip. Some were close ups, some from distance. He had film from all angles. Each repetition from training was followed up with a game clip showing the transfer of sled work to reality. The sequencing was brilliantly organized. It started with a perfect finished product. Clips of full speed forearm Crowther style blocking from stance through footwork, to blow delivery, leg drive, follow through, and finish. To see it done well is a thing of beauty, like watching most masters perform their craft — it all looks so easy.

> **Always start with a perfect end picture. Find the
> very best there is to watch, study, and learn from.
> Make sure it's clear, understood, and burned deep.**

The tape ran on, breaking the block down into segments. The fit of the forearm into the pad, followed up with a game clip of that same perfect forearm placement into a live defender. Then, the perfect lunge step that accompanies the forearm blow, again followed up with seeing it transfer to reality, and on and on. The objective here was to introduce the style of blocking we would learn. Dan had specifically chosen plays that showed the technique being performed as perfectly as possible. It was my first experience with this, and he knew the power of initial impressions — the power of creating a perfect visual for me to work from.

The Power of Visualization

Dan initiated this learning by helping me visualize the end picture, and I've never forgotten those clips. They became the picture in my mind that we worked on painting every day. It was the visual framework to help guide me through all the frustrating physical work we were about to do. I could clearly SEE the goal. I had a clear picture of where I was going. Without a clear end picture, how do you know if you're heading in the right direction? Dan made sure we started there, he knew the power of starting with a great vison. This became a pattern for the rest of my career. Any new technique or scheme always began by viewing it being done as perfectly as possible. The initial impression mattered. I can't count how many clips I watched of Jeff Saturday, Bryan Chiu, Kevin Mawae, and countless other great centers performing seemingly flawless form with techniques Dan was going to work with me on. Those images set the visual standard for me to work from.

The Takeaway

Dan made sure that I saw what the end product should look like. That's a lesson I have always remembered and continually utilize today. They say your thoughts dictate your action. Dan knew the importance of building a great mental picture — one that would focus my thoughts and guide my actions. That's the best place to start. I learned quickly, though, that it was far easier to see it done right than personally doing it well.

HUMOR, NOT HUMILIATION

"A sense of humor is part of the art of leadership, of getting along with people, of getting things done."

~ Dwight D. Eisenhower

Dan had a great sense of humor and understood the importance of **earning the right** to poke fun at somebody, but he didn't form a relationship in that manner. I never once saw Dan take the bully stance and initiate a player relationship with teasing. That's an old school macho alpha play that is not only childish but screams of insecurity. Dan was too much of a gentleman for that nonsense. He first made sure he had earned that right by getting to know you and having been through some battles with you.

Humor Never Came Before Trust

Poking fun at somebody was a privilege that needed to be earned, and that was a huge lesson for me. You had to have a level of trust first, so that any teasing could be laughed off by both parties with the confidence and certainty that there is no deeper power play at hand.

Don't Poke Mama Bear

Mid-way through my first year, I gave up a bad sack against the Ottawa Renegades. It wasn't a mental mistake or an inability to recognize or pick up a twist. This was one of those sacks where you got flat out beat one on one. One of those sacks that takes zero football knowledge to know what just happened. I got whooped.

I learned later in my career not to listen to the post-game show on my drive home. In my first few years, though, I was a glutton for punishment. We had won, which usually meant positive call ins. Still, there's always somebody that needs to vent. *"We need to get rid of Reid!"* The caller said it with such anger that you would've thought I had just stolen his life savings. He was genuinely mad. *"He's too small! He can't hold his own. He's gotta go!"* I probably would've forgotten that call except for what happened next.

"And next, we have Alicia calling from Richmond. What did you think about tonight's game, Alicia?" NO WAY! NO WAY this is MY MOM calling in! Please NO! Sure enough, it was. *"I think that last caller is an idiot. My boy Angus is the best center in the league. That nose guard was a dirty player. He was going after my boy's knees all game. He should have been penalized for dirty play!"* Okay...did that just happen? Did my mom really just call in on the post-game show to stand up for me? Sure did. I really wonder if that has ever happened before or after in the entire world of all professional sports — a mom calling in to defend her son and blasting a caller right after they hang up. I was so embarrassed. At least I was on my way home already, and the probability of anyone else on my team ever hearing that would be as Dan would say, *"Slim to none, and Slim just left town."*

This was 2003, long before social media or any other platform existed for someone to grab that snippet and spread it like wildfire. It happened, it was embarrassing, but it was over. No one that matters heard it and it will never be heard again, I can move on.

Full of Surprises

Film the next day was fine. I actually played a pretty solid game, save that one embarrassing blemish. I knew it was coming, and I was prepared accordingly. I knew we'd have to dissect all that I did wrong. The point would also be made loud and clear that "some people" can get away with sloppy technique from time to time, but I was in no way one of those people.

Just as my garbage play was about to begin, Dan's cell phone rang. Two things shocked me:

1. That Dan would break a team rule and leave his cell phone on during a team meeting.
2. That Dan HAD a cell phone!

Dan may be one of the most technologically inefficient people I have ever met. He not only wrote out our scouting reports by hand, but he also used those old school drafting sets to trace out each individual circle and square to draw our blocking schemes in the reports. Think about that for a second. Each play would have at least 12 circles and 12 squares. There were dozens of plays for each game prep. That is a ton of meticulous time spent on something that technology and the press of a computer bottom had made unnecessary years and years earlier. Dan never seemed to care, though. He had no need for modern technology or the efficiencies it offered. He was old school in every respect. So, realizing Dan had a cell phone in 2003 was odd enough. Why the call came through was another shock entirely.

"Hello! Oh, hi Mrs. Reid! Good to hear from you."

Wait. What? My mom?

"Oh, don't you worry, Mrs. Reid. Your boy is in good hands. We will make sure no dirty nose guard goes after his knees ever again."

The issue for me in that moment was that I knew my mother very well. There was a very real chance that, somehow, she actually was calling. As crazy at that sounds, she'd done crazier. Dan kept this going for a few more minutes. He never once made eye contact with me. He stayed sternly focused on his phone interaction. Always focused on his direct task. He finally concluded the call by thanking her for reaching out and telling her to please call anytime. The room was silent. I was sure not one other person in there had heard her call the show the night before. I was sure of it. Boy, was I wrong.

Word Travels Fast

Our veteran right tackle had heard exactly what I had. He was the kind of guy that relished any opportunity to tease a fellow teammate and create a good laugh for all. Turns out, he'd set the whole thing up. Dan was in on it since early that morning. They had our quarterback Dave Dickenson call Dan at the exact time Dan had instructed him to. It was all orchestrated to be timed right to that play — precision in everything he did, even his humor. Dan closed the phone, flashed me a grin, and the room erupted. Everyone knew! Dan had meticulously planned this like he planned everything. Nothing Dan did was random, not even this. He then went right back to the film and critiquing my "lack of anchor" on the sack, pointing out all the things I failed to do to recover from my poor form. That was that.

The Takeaway

Humor is such a strong tool. It can help cut tension, dial down anxiety, and humanize relationships, especially in a coaching / evaluating type environment. As a player, you become hyper-aware of every word a coach says. Without humor, the exchanges become purely clinical, the same corrections and phrasing heard again and again. Dan was the greatest I had ever seen at removing the player from the performance. That was key. It allowed him to criticize the act, not the person. Sometimes, though, you need to be reminded that you're still human. You need to know someone cares about you more than just how your body moved on film.

LEARNING IN REVERSE

"Bottle that up and put a cap on it!"

~ **Dan**

"Ready…HIT…HOLD…PRONATE…PRONATE!"

Dan repeated this endlessly during every Crowther training session throughout my entire career. I began a measured arms-length away from the 3'–4' long vertically curved pad on the sled. From a semi squat athletic stance, I was positioned, splitting the foot-wide pad to the right of my groin. On the "HIT!" command, I was to launch my right forearm into the curve of the pad, horizontally, as if violently raising a shield into an oncoming attacker, striking deep into the pad, and connecting with a strong "Thud!" Then the command of "HOLD!" I had to hold this finished position, maintaining full tension throughout my entire body while Dan went to work correcting the problems.

The corrections came with cues. He rotated my thumb downwards, pushing more of the meaty side of my forearm into the pad of the sled. Once he was happy with placement and rotation, he went to work on tucking my elbow back inside the framework of my torso. *"No chicken wings!"* he'd bark, in reference to my elbow initially sticking way out to the side. Everything needed to end up inside the framework of my body.

"We want all your force to go THOUGH the defender. Anything sticking out to the side will bleed force with it."

Constructive Criticism with Purpose

Dan never corrected anything without a very thorough explanation of why. Everything had a reason. Again, tinkering away, he meticulously aligned every part of my body to where it should end up. Once he had constructed the perfect finished product, he had me maintain that pose for just a bit longer.

"Hold...HOOOOLD...BREAK!"

The "BREAK!" was always accompanied with a sharp slap on my rear end, giving me the green light to relax. The hold was important for three reasons:

1. He needed time to correct me and get everything aligned perfectly.

2. He needed to expose my weak points to find where and what was limiting me from getting into the perfect position. Tight areas in my body were usually preventing me from achieving perfect form. (It was almost always tight hip flexors.)

3. He wanted me to FEEL perfect form. Watching someone do it on film is one thing; learning to feel it is another. You need to learn to FEEL perfect form. Perfect position with strong tension holds are a great and safe way to build that kinesthetic awareness of what you want your body to do.

Dysfunction Will Always Be a Hindrance

I learned two important rules long ago from strength coaches I admire greatly:

1. Never add speed to dysfunction

2. Never add load to dysfunction

Master the positioning and function before you start adding speed or load. That's how Dan always taught. Everything was reverse engineered. The finished position was worked on first, then backwards we went.

Once I had mastered the technique and placement of my forearm thud into the pad, it was time to add the hips. Starting from the same measured distance, I was now to initiate my forearm blow by thrusting my hips forward. Basically, broad jumping out. The only difference being my forearm connecting violently into the pad prevented my body from really propelling anywhere. This is where you really started to see what you were doing. This is the movement chunk that started to expose anything that wasn't done just right.

Going Old School

Of the hundreds and hundreds of equipment options coaches can use, Dan put the Crowther sled above them all. There was a simple reason: it acted as Dan would often say, as an "analytical computer." It gave you instant feedback. It allowed no room for error and was embarrassingly unforgiving. If you didn't hit it exactly right, it did all kinds of goofy things…except slide back. If you hit it too high, the back end would spike down and stop you right in your tracks. If you weren't aligned right and bled some of your force anywhere but directly through it, it would spin like a top, leaving you flat on your face. It was a tough buck to master. It required detailed examination of what you were doing. Perfection of movement was your only option to gain its approval. There was no way to fool the sled. You had to hit it right.

The hip thrust, if done right, usually ended up with a nice "POP" sound of your forearm hitting the pad. The spring-loaded pad absorbs the blow, coils and releases, sliding the entire sled back a few feet. The sliding creates enough space for your hips to finish extending fully, allowing you to gently fall to the ground on your chest and face. As with most things, when done right, it feels so good. When done anything but just right, it's a mess. I seemed to get the static hip thrust, forearm blow chunk down pretty fast. For me, it was a weight room power clean — a motion I'd mastered years earlier. Then, we moved backwards again.

Dan would always remind us that the hip thrust generates the force behind the blow delivery…but it's the legs that get you there and keep you going after impact. From that same arms-length measured distance, I now had the ability to generate power from my hips, but this time I had to propel one leg out at the same time as my forearm. Always the same arm, same leg. There are physics and power ratio purposes at play there that are way beyond my pay grade. Trust in my coach and tangible results from that trust were enough for me. More importantly, though, opposite leg to arm just simply wouldn't work. That's really all I needed to know. The forearm would connect just a split second before the foot would drive into the ground. If done right, the right forearm would thud powerfully deep into the curve of the pad just as the right foot connected to the ground. The pad would slide back a bit, creating enough space to fully finish the hip extension, leaving me in a somewhat extreme lunge-like position. I really sucked at this one.

Maybe it was my tight hips, or maybe I simply struggled to get properly aligned. Whatever the reason, this chunk of the movement routinely gave me fits. The sled would always spin on contact, yet Dan would still make me hold while he looked to correct and rebuild my form (even though half the time I was trying to keep from falling on my face because I had lost all contact with the stupid sled that spun away). That thing would not cut me a break, and it always revealed the truth. It seemed like we worked on that movement forever. I was not fast to pick that one up. Keeping in line with basic training principles of not adding speed or load to dysfunction, that is where we stayed. I know Dan wanted to get to the full block and to start adding movement in my stance, but that would've just been wrong.

You Don't Add Floors to a House When Its Foundation Isn't Solid

It took forever, but I finally got it. It was both embarrassing and frustrating to struggle with this seemingly simple movement. Whatever frustration Dan may have inwardly felt, outwardly he only projected concern for my improvement. Helping instruct, correct, and sometimes simply encouraging me to keep my focus and to keep at it. Never once did Dan lay into me for "not getting it." That would have served no productive purpose. **If the words don't help, don't say them.** His only verbal expression of frustration came from lack of effort. Luckily for me, that was the one area I could give Dan absolute confidence in. The rest, well, he kept those frustrations to himself. He just kept "coaching my ass off."

The Lunge Step Accomplishment

It took a while for me to master that stupid lunge step portion of the Crowther block, but I finally did. Just like when I mastered any other segment of any other skill, Dan would finish on that rep with his all too familiar, *"Bottle that one up and put a cap on it."* He always wanted me to end on a great rep. He knew both the psychological and physical benefit of finishing on your very best effort. The last rep is the one that stays with you. The last rep is the place you pick up from next time. Once you've done it great, stop there, bottle it up, put a cap on it, and save it for next time.

Dan never wanted us to regress or let our technique get sloppy from repetition just for repetition's sake. The point was to learn a skill, not to build toughness or endurance – that's what the box and all his other crazy workouts were for. Skill building was about detail. It was about getting to that perfect movement and stopping, then coming back to it again the next time. Then, when you've done it just right again, stop. Slowly with time, the body recognizes that perfect motion and learns to adapt to that as being how it should always do it. It's painfully slow sometimes getting to that place of great technique, but once there, you'd do yourself a disservice by over-repping to the point of compromising form due to fatigue. It was a fine line, one that Dan walked very cautiously on. Conditioning was one thing; learning perfect form was another. One, he pushed my physical limits with, the other, he did everything he could to avoid exhaustion.

The Pleasure of Perfection

From there, the rest of it rolled smoothly. I went from two step contact, then backed out again and started coming out of my stance. When we finally got to the place where he had me do the block full speed, from stance through to finish, I got it the very first time. It looked like I had been doing this block my whole life. It felt easy, powerful, and smooth. I 'felt' like the vison he had me burned into my brain from all that film study. I 'felt' my body moving through all the positions he had me hold and correct and hold again until I was aligned just right. Each feeling was engrained. I had built that block piece by piece — each step mastered from three separate, yet mutually important, parts:

1. External feedback and physical corrections from my coach — right there on the spot.

2. External feedback from the equipment being used — instant, objective, and always consistent.

3. My internal mapping of feeling all the corrections and feeling and learning from the equipment feedback.

The Benefits and Limitations of Film

We did end up using film from time to time. That allowed us to review from a different vantage point. For me, to see what I looked like, and from a coach's view, to see how things looked and where improvements could be made. Film has become the accepted gold standard in coaching and teaching things. There is tremendous value in being able to see what you looked like while performing. To see the difference between what you thought you were doing compared to what you actually did. Sometimes, that difference can be shocking, usually in a humbling way. There's an old saying that you're never as good as you think you are, and you're probably not as bad as you might think you are either. Film is pretty good at showing you the truth, which tends to lie somewhere in between.

As good as film is, the ability to 'feel' the corrections in the movement, I have found always translates better to changing your actions in that moment. When the speed of the game or real-life kicks in, you revert to habits. Those habits need to be built, perfected, and rehearsed again and again until you don't have to think your way through them anymore. Your instincts become the movement that has been coached into you. Your body does what feels right because that is the motion it has been exposed to so many times that it accepts it as the most efficient way to move.

"Get comfortable being uncomfortable" – Dan

Practicing Discomfort

The funny thing about offensive linemen is that every single thing we do out there is contrary to what our bodies naturally want to do. Unlike so many other athletic movements, like sprinting and jumping, offensive linemen fight their bodies every step of the way. Dan would constantly remind me that *"Great offensive lineman train themselves to be comfortable being uncomfortable." "Think about it,"* he would go on,

"You spend your whole lives in a squat position; nobody wants to live down there. It hurts; it burns. Your body is begging you to just stand up and get comfortable...but that's when you lose." It was a comforting feeling to know that my advantage was found in my ability to be uncomfortable longer than my opponent. *"**He who stays lower longer wins**"* was a saying that has never left me. It's about the power of delayed gratification, the ability to hold out just a bit longer, to avoid the pleading temptation to relax and get comfortable. That's what winning the game of blocking is all about. That's what really winning in life is all about. Trust in the technique you've been taught, then have the patience and guts to live in that trained uncomfortable state longer than your opponent. That takes more than a mindset. That takes serious training. That takes getting and keeping your body or mind in that perfectly aligned position again and again until that uncomfortable state becomes your new accepted norm. The beautiful thing is, once you've reached that state, it becomes hard to live your life any other way.

The Takeaway

It's tempting to just keep going, to avoid working on the parts you're struggling with. Speed can sometimes mask issues, for a while at least. After all, it's frustrating to stay at the basics. But what isn't started right, can't end right. What isn't built right, ultimately won't perform right. It takes whatever time it takes. You can't skip steps because they're hard or because you suck at them. That way of going about learning will bite you in the ass when it matters most.

TRAINING CAMP
The Value of Visuals and Repetition

"Championships are not won on Grey Cup Sunday; they are won at training camp."

~ **Dan**

Dan asked if I would come to rookie camp that year. I was technically a third-year vet so by no means obligated to go, but I had very little real playing experience and a whole new system to learn. I thought it would be great to get a head start on the vets, particularly because entering camp I was the de facto starting center since Jamie Taras had retired at the end of last season. They had brought in a veteran American and drafted a young center to compete, but the notion seemed to be the job was mine if I could perform to expectations. Because I had spent the most time with Dan that off-season, I became his demo go-to guy for drill and technique teaching. I relished the role and felt great confidence throughout those long rookie camp two-a-day practices. For the first time in my pro career, I felt like I belonged. I had a coach that used me as the example of how to do things. What a difference a year can make. I was a leader during those three days. Finally, I had arrived.

Then the vets showed up. Real camp was about to start. Things were about to get serious.

Always Start with the Big Picture:
Dan on Having and Seeing Your Philosophy

"Five Guys – One Heartbeat"

Main Camp – Part Reunion, Part Stare Down

The first evening of main camp is always an interesting time. It's a bizarre combination of vets exchanging welcoming laughs and hugs after a long off-season apart, and rookies and other newbies peacocking as best they can to make sure you respect their presence. I understood it but always found it strange, like we've never really changed from our school yard days. All the laughter and posturing goes away quickly after the initial welcome back meal and intro full team meeting.

Dan understood all too well the power of environment. The feeling you get from your physical surroundings will always have at least some impact on your emotional frame of mind. He did what he could to make our offensive line meeting room as psychologically empowering as possible. No matter where we were, he tried to make our meeting space feel special. Even in a makeshift room on the main floor of our training camp hotel in beautiful Chilliwack, British Columbia.

During rookie camp, the normally bland ballroom was transformed into an offensive lineman's den of inspiration. He had these huge quote boards made. They surrounded nearly every open space, leaving no way to escape the powerful statements reminding us of who we were and what we were there to do. "FIVE GUYS, ONE HEART." "FIVE FINGERS, ONE GLOVE" They went on and on. It was as if we were reading a wall-sized motivational quote book for offensive linemen. They never ended, and each year Dan seemed to just add to the list. It got to the point where he had so many that he had to start rotating them weekly. The phrases may have been never ending, but unfortunately the wall space was not.

By the end of the three-day rookie camp, that room had already grown on me. Maybe it was because I felt confident being the "veteran" rookie of the bunch or that my three days were going well. Either way, and for whatever reason, it felt like home…then all the real vets came piling in. All of a sudden, my seniority confidence dropped a few floors, and I found myself quietly looking for a new seat.

Everything in the room looked exactly the same…except for what was paused on the big screen. For the rest of my career, the only thing that was ever paused, waiting for us on the big screen, was football. Always something football. It may have been a play from a game, a practice, or just a drill, but it was always football. Except this one time. Dan's first ever full group meeting as the offensive line coach for the British Columbia Lions started off with a full projector-sized picture of a big pot belly pig. I will never forget that image as long as I live. How could I? What was this guy up to? Dan just proved he already knew how to grab our attention.

Visually Know Your Philosophy

Most people would've addressed the absurdity of the image in some way. As I was already learning, Dan is not most people. He greeted us all with a warm welcome, thanked us all for committing our time and energy to trying to help this club win, commented on the great work we had already put in, and then got right down to it.

"Offensive linemen are not like other athletes. We do things most people would not or could not do."

His speech was just how I had come to learn it. Slow, controlled, deliberate, yet intense.

"I want you to take great pride in that fact."

He had a way of instilling confidence in you long before any action had ever been taken. He always used words to reiterate his pride and appreciation for us and our commitment to the work ahead.

"We don't move like other athletes."

He then pointed to the giant pig.

"We plot…always balanced…always strong on our feet."

I was still waiting for a buildup to a punch line. Not today. He was actually serious.

"Like this big guy here."

He kept his finger rigidly pointed at the sow.

"We work and live with a low center of gravity and push things out of our way."

I had already been exposed to Dan's belief in the power of images; I had just never seen him use them for an abstract concept before. He was visually building our philosophy of what it conceptually meant to be an offensive lineman. Most people would view being called a pig an insult, but Dan saw the species as a beautiful example of what you want to be more like – on the football field, at least.

"How does this look in action?"

Dan turned away from the screen and stared directly at us. His big eyebrows jumped as if looking for a response, but he wasn't. It was just part of the dramatic effect he used to emphasize a rhetorical question that he would answer momentarily. He clicked his film "cowboy," (coach lingo for a remote control) and the screen jumped from the charming swine to a sumo wrestling match. He broke down the match as if reviewing a play. First, he let the tape run, which was just enough time for us to really begin questioning why we were watching it. Then he spoke.

"Let's study this for sec, shall we?"

Then it got a little weird. He began breaking down the match with the same extreme detail he did for each and every one of our plays. Pause, rewind, pause, rewind, pause. Each stop was at a different moment to break down and discuss a different segment of their movement.

"You see that right there?"

He paused as the two giants were initiating contact with each other. Again, it was rhetorical, which was great because I really wasn't certain about the answer he was looking for. I had never before, or again in my life, broken down a sumo wrestling match. All I saw were two massive men wearing something resembling a cloth diaper, charging at each other.

"Look there."

He now had his laser pointer out, directing our eyes exactly where he wanted them to look.

"You see the difference?"

He was now bouncing the laser back and forth between the two giants' stomachs. Specifically, the exact middle of their stomachs. Their center of gravity. These guys were both huge, make no mistake about that, but one was significantly bigger than the other. In a sport where size is prized above all, you would think the bigger man would always win. Not so. It was the much smaller man whose center of gravity was lower on impact that won — not because he was a tad shorter, but because his legs were bent more.

"This little guy's gonna win."

Little, as I came to learn all too well in my career, is a very relative word. Dan was fired up now, like he was about to win a bet or something.

"You know why?"

His eyes lit up, and his eyebrows nearly jumped off his face.

"Because he's a knee bender!"

He said it with the intensity and volume one not knowing him would mistake for anger. This was his big punch line. He let the tape run, and we watched what Dan had predicted. The "little" guy drove the bigger man right out of the circle.

"Men…" He slowed his voice and quieted his volume. *"That's what we do. You are all big men but being big is not enough. We win because of how you train yourself to move. How you train your body to be stronger than your opponent's. It's technique; it's leverage, and it's what an offensive lineman is all about."*

Dan went on for a bit, wanting to make the point very clear that winning at our position was not a result of just being bigger than the other guy. It was a result of the discipline needed to train our bodies to move in an unnatural, mostly uncomfortable way, better and longer than our opponents.

Have a Mission Statement

That video sort of set the tone. For many of the vets, those first 10 minutes of animal farm and ABC's Wide World of Sports was their very first exposure to Dan. Many of them did not live here in the off-season and hadn't been exposed to his off-season torture sessions like I had been. If I was surprised with his meeting opening, I could only imagine what some of those other guys were thinking. I'm fairly certain Dan had firmly grabbed their attention, if for nothing more than curiosity of what he might show them next.

He clicked his "cowboy," and the screen changed to something much more pedestrian. Words.

OUR PLAN

1. **TO BE A PHYSICAL OFFENSIVE LINE**
2. **TO HAVE A GREAT WORK ETHIC**
3. **TO PLAY WITH INTELLIGENCE**
4. **TO BE A MASTERPIECE IN PRECISION**
5. **TO HAVE A TEAM ATTITUDE**

This list became both our group philosophy and mission statement. It encompassed the type of offensive line we would always strive to be. I didn't realize it in that moment, but the power of actually defining who you are, what you stand for, and what you are constantly striving to be, is one of the most powerful things you can ever do. It becomes the bullseye you're gunning for. It guides every decision and action moving forward. For Dan, this became the measuring stick to gauge our actions. Was what we were doing supporting these five beliefs or not? Were our actions as a group in line with our plan? It gave great clarity to the otherwise murky question of "who are you?" This was who we were, or at least constantly striving to be. The most empowering aspect of this list was that each point was, for the most part, within our control. These were not outcome-oriented statements. These were behavior measurables. We could always strive to live these five points at any time. It was an outline of how we were to choose going about playing this position. No talent needed for that.

> **Clarity of purpose is such a powerful thing.**

Making It Stick

Dan talked through the mostly self-explanatory points and added his own thoughts on each. Making the list is easy — it's the buy-in and follow through that actually mean something. This list became not only the discussion point for the next 20 minutes but also a fixture in every meeting room we ever had to use (home or away), and more importantly was included on every single piece of game prep literature we had issued to us for the remainder of my career. You couldn't get away from it. Constant visual repetition is a powerful thing. I've looked at those five points so many times that I can rattle them off in my sleep. They weren't read and forgotten. They were emphasized and reiterated everywhere to the point that you couldn't forget them even if you tried. Once that happens, it's in you; it's part of you. When you get to that point, words on a screen turn into real life actions. We didn't always live up to those five points, but I can promise you, it wasn't because we were ever unclear about them.

The Takeaway

That day, Dan was speaking to us as a group, but I left believing he was sharing a personal reminder with me directly. Great speakers tend to have that skill. I may very well have been the smallest one in that room and routinely the smallest lineman in the league, but that was not going to be an excuse. Size was helpful for sure, but when it came right down to it, you win because of leverage and technique.

Dan used visuals to express the baseline philosophy of the what, how, and why we do what we do, and the fact that this is a position that rewards discipline of bodily control and technique. The images of that pig and those sumo wrestlers are forever cemented in my memory, far clearer than any words have even been. His 10-minute visual presentation did more to clarify philosophically who we were and how we do things better than anything I have heard or studied since. Simple. Clear. Powerful. Effective.

Dan taught me the power of not just clearly defining who you are and what that means, but to keep that close at hand. To review it constantly until it is engrained to the point that it is always with you, always reminding you, and always guiding you.

ON EXCUSES

"I don't want to hear them – do your job."

~ **Dan**

"But, Dan, I tripped!"

Everything after that went silent. Dan just stared at me with that look of disbelief. He could really over-dramatize his facial expressions. I mean, he put this look on thick. You would've thought I had just told a young child that there was no Santa Claus. He held that look on purpose. He wanted to make a visual point before he addressed me verbally. The silence gave all 11 or so other linemen in the room time to realize I had obviously said something very stupid and was about to be used to address something very important. I had no idea what that knee jerk reactionary comment would trigger, but the silence and expression on Dan's face left me wishing I could reach out, collect those words, and shove them back into my big mouth. In the end, I'm happy I couldn't. What Dan went into next altered how I viewed what I did and the accountability I would take for my actions moving forward.

"Angus…" He finally broke the silence. Of course, he followed my name with another long pause. *"Let me tell you something. In life, there will always be reasons for what happened. There are NEVER any excuses. We can work with reasons. We can improve and correct them. Excuses? I don't want to hear them – EVER. They serve no productive purpose."* We all know this, but it's hard sometimes to remember. Then another short pause.

"Hold on a second!" Now, he seemed fired up. He flashed a look at his watch, jumped his eyes back to us, then, almost daringly shouted *"TIME ME,"* and off he went. I mean it. He just took off. I'd never seen anything like it before. I would say also since, but remember, I played 10 more seasons with Dan.

Nobody actually timed him. I mean, seriously, come on. Dan returned at the same speed he left us – FULL. He was gone for exactly 2 minutes and 18 seconds. How do I know? Because he timed himself! He was never one to waste anything, especially time, and in particular that of others. He noted that meetings would be ending 2 minutes and 18 seconds earlier today. True Dan…never one to take anything without giving it back.

He also held something in his hand…a single piece of transparent paper. This was projector material stuff. This was important — his 12 unacceptable excuses were now glowing bright on the wall before us.

EXCUSES

1. I THOUGHT…
2. YEAH, BUT…
3. I DID WHAT YOU TOLD ME TO DO, BUT IT DIDN'T WORK.
4. I'LL GET HIM IN THE GAME!
5. I SLIPPED!
6. I TRIPPED!
7. THE BACK KNOCKED ME OFF!
8. I IDIDN'T HEAR THE AUDIBLE!
9. SEEMED LIKE A GOOD THING TO DO AT THE TIME!
10. I FORGOT!
11. I DIDN'T UNDERSTAND YOUR INSTRUCTIONS!
12. I HAVE THE WRONG SHOES ON.

Dan made it easy to remember things. Rules. Lists of Rules. Clear, concise rules. Once taught, he would repeat and reinforce often. He knew the power of repetition for not only physical technique work, but also mental habitual training. This list became our no-fly zone. No matter what went wrong on a play, you were never allowed to use any of these 12 phrases – EVER.

We went back to the film. It was time to emphasize his point even more. He rolled back the play I tripped on.

"Angus, you did indeed trip. The question is why."

I was trying to get to my second level block and tripped over my right guard's ankle. I had seen it merely as something that 'sometimes just happens.' That thinking removed any responsibility and removed any learning potential. Dan wouldn't allow that.

"Study your footwork…study it closely."

Okay, this really sucked. Dan was now getting the entire room to break down in great detail minute issues with my footwork technique. With the focus set on why it happened, it became painfully clear that my footwork was a tad sloppy, not terrible, but a 'crisper' technique with less 'loping steps,' as Dan would call them, would have prevented the entanglement.

It took maybe 10 minutes (including Dan's 2:18 shuttle run), but his lecture and lesson on refusing to accept excuses and the danger they present to learning stuck.

> **Never again would I cling to the reason itself as an excuse.
> The reason became the study point to learn more about
> what I was doing and how I could improve because of it.**

The Takeaway

Dan challenged us to never again lean on excuses and to stop outsourcing the responsibilities of our actions. He forced us to face them, to search and find answers, to study, learn, and grow from what happened.

I hung around after meetings that day. I wanted to thank Dan for making it very clear the pointlessness of going to excuses. What he said in that short 5-minute chat left me with a framework and a phrase that I have never forgotten.

"Let me tell you something Angus…"

I learned to love chats with Dan that started this way. It always felt like a movie scene where a father was about to dive into a deep heart to heart with his son.

> **"A good carpenter never blames his tools."**

I had never heard that saying before, but I instantly loved it. It has never left me.

"I got no time for excuses. You either did your job or you didn't. There is nobody else to blame. Get away from excuses, and we can get on with improving."

CHOOSING MY FOCUS

"You are where you place your focus."

~ **Dan**

"You've got to be kidding me! This is not happening." In my entire sporting life since I was a fifth grader, I had never done this. Now, here I was, 34 years old, in the visitor's locker room at Commonwealth Stadium in Edmonton digging through my travel bag with the false sense of hope I may have the other one — knowing full well I didn't.

We had flown into Edmonton the day before but had chosen not to go to the stadium for a short walk-through. A few times in my career we skipped that step, opting instead for longer meetings and more rest. That little scheduling tweak ended up putting me in a pickle of my own doing. We had to be at the stadium a minimum of two and a half hours before kickoff. That was our team rule, and the chartered bus would pick everyone up from the hotel accordingly. You had all the freedom in the world to get to the stadium anyway you liked, but two and a half hours prior to kickoff, you better be in the building. Official warmups didn't start until fifty minutes prior to kickoff. That gave you some solid time to prepare as you felt fit. Lots of guys got ready super early. I'm talking two and sometimes two and a half hours pre-game. They go out on the field half-dressed and go through whatever their pre-game ritual may be.

Not me, probably due to Dan's training and my general desire not to waste energy running around until absolutely needed. That being said, I always opted to be at the stadium early. Usually three hours prior. That gave me a solid 30 minutes to enjoy the quiet of an empty stadium before the madness started to build. I loved that feeling of a stadium at peace. It was a relaxing time to enjoy a coffee, joke with our equipment and medical staff, and generally enjoy some final mental and physical rest before battle.

Because I wasn't into elaborate warmups, I rarely got dressed early. I didn't get much of my body taped up either. I was very low maintenance — just the way I liked it. Not needing much, leaving not much to need, and ideally leaving very little to go wrong. Even still, there are a few things that are essential. With 60 minutes 'til kickoff and 10 until we had to go out for warmup, I had just realized I was missing one of those very few, but very much needed, essential items – a right shoe!

I had broken two cardinal rules that trip:

1. I hadn't double checked my shoes before packing them.

2. I hadn't packed a second pair of shoes.

What I HAD done was pack two left shoes! I'd become careless and forgotten a basic lesson learned from Dan regarding calling defenses. Use the checklist EVERY SINGLE TIME. Don't get lazy and skip steps. You never know when that skipped step will bite you. I got lazy when packing. I just grabbed two and chucked them in. That laziness was now biting me – hard. I knew our equipment staff always travelled with a few extra pairs 'just in case,' but I also knew that none of those shoes would work. My shattered foot in '09 had left me with a largely lumped right hoof. So much so that no regular shoe would fit properly. I was only an 11 ½, but my right foot now needed closer to a 12 ½ in order to get over the bulged scar tissue arcing over the top. Our equipment manager had found me some Nikes that were uniquely cut to be way wider right where I needed them to be. They fit like a glove. He had gotten me two pairs, and I couldn't have been happier. I knew for a fact he hadn't ordered three. That meant there was no way there would just happen to be an extra pair lying around in the equipment bag. I was the only one on the team with these shoes. Right then, though, I was the only one on the team who didn't have shoes! I panicked.

The Only Player with Fred Flintstone's Feet

Almost all the lineman on our team had feet that were at least size 14. Most were 15s, some even bigger. I might as well have borrowed Ronald McDonald's shoes. That wasn't going to work. The players in my size range were receivers and running backs and such. Almost all wore low cuts and had these light, narrow, track style boots designed for speed, not support. As the clock ticked down, so did my options.

No Good Answer for A Self-Inflicted Problem

I finally compromised and borrowed a pair from our All-Star defensive end Keron Williams. Keron was a stud. He played the part and looked it, too, right down to his footwear. I slid right into those smooth black patent leather Nikes. They were so sweet! I guarantee you they were not created or designed to ever have an offensive lineman wear them. They were high cuts, which was the good part. The bad part? They were size 13 ½. Way too big! They were the closest I could get, and we were heading out for kickoff in two minutes. I was seriously stressed.

There was a bigger issue at hand as well. We were entering this game 1–6. It had been the very worst start that I had ever been a part of. We were terrible, and our rope had run out. We had a bye week following this game, and it had been made very clear that without some miracle, major changes were going to be made. I was 34, over-age, and over paid. I knew where the first cuts would come from. With so much on the line, all I could do was stress over these shoes that no matter how tight I tied them up were way too big for me. The shoes were all I could think about.

Dan's Wisdom

Thankfully, my mind shifted to three things Dan would harp on again and again and again.

1. You become where you place your focus and attention. This was repeated often and usually in the context of blocking defenders. He always stressed that where our eyes go, our focus goes, and so do our hands and ultimately our bodies. Where you put your attention dictates where you are and where you will end up.

2. Dan's list of unacceptable excuses.

3. Having the wrong shoes on was the last item on that list.

Finding My Focus

Those three thoughts flashed through my mind, but I was a professional and had a job to do. That's what mattered. That's where my focus had to be, so that's where I put it. I promised myself right in that moment that I wouldn't think about my shoes ever again that day. That promise would have held true, too, but as I should have guessed, shoes like that on a guy like me don't stay unnoticed for very long.

As I also should have guessed, it would be Dan's eye for detail that not only picked up on the oddity, but he also had a sarcastic comment already lined up. All I heard as I jogged past him getting ready to fall in line for team warmups was a slight mocking yet puzzled sounding jab.

"You wearing your dancing shoes today, Angus?"

Without breaking stride or even turning back, I proudly threw back at him, *"These are my ass kicking shoes, coach. Came to kick some ass today."* That was it. Not one more thought ever went to those massively oversized, completely out of place looking sleek Nike Speed TD cleats.

You are where you place your attention. I shifted mine from an excuse to the mission at hand — to doing my job. That's exactly what I went out and did. My actions followed my focus. I played one of my best games that season. Grading out at 96%. We destroyed Edmonton that day 36–1. We not only saved all of our careers but put in motion that day the beginnings of the greatest turn around in professional football history. We went on to go 9–1 the rest of the year en route to winning the Grey Cup in our home stadium. We became the first team in professional football history to start a season 1–6 that went on to win the championship. That magical season will never be forgotten. What probably will by everyone except myself is that I could have easily tanked that day. I could have easily allowed my careless blunder to create a distraction and a preprogrammed excuse that would have distracted me, shifting my attention away from my job and directed it solely to problem. Thankfully, I didn't. Dan's constant reminders of his refusal to accept excuses and the power of where your focus goes saved me that day.

The Takeaway

That critical game not only saved that season, but maybe my career as well. I never again allowed my focus to shift to issues that were pressing to pull my attention away from what really mattered. I also never again forgot to diligently doublecheck my packing.

ON SEEING BOTH THE FOREST AND THE TREES

"To play offensive line, you need to have great spatial focus."

~ Dan

I kept waiting for Dan to slap me. Slap me hard. Right in the face. I was supposed to be focusing on the "IO" of the "BC LIONS" screen-printed across the chest of his team-issued shirt, but my mind kept drifting back to a scene from Rocky II. Rocky had gone to see his old manager Mickey late one night to try to convince him he could still fight. Mickey, wanting to protect the long-term health of his beat-up fighter, had to prove a point. He had Rocky stare right at his nose – with all his focus. He held his left-hand way off to the side and wanted Rocky to let him know the second he could see it in his periphery without adjusting his focus on Mick's nose one bit. He caught the left hand early. Mickey was pleased. The right hand was a different story. Some heavy damage had compromised the vison in Rocky's right eye. He had no chance. He didn't see a thing. It's funny how sometimes your memory makes up its own reality.

In the actual scene, Mickey explains that Apollo Creed would have just caved in his face by now. He did end up slapping Rocky a few moments later to prove his point. For whatever reason, that's all I could think of — a memory from a movie I had watched way too many times as a kid (incorrectly remembering the scene). The mind can be funny like that sometimes.

Dan didn't slap me, thankfully. Even though I think those first two or three workouts he could easily have, and I wouldn't have seen it coming either. My focus wasn't yet at a level that it needed to be.

Focus Is Everything

Focus was what mattered most to Dan. It all started with the placement of your eyes. Dan would forever remind us that "where your eyes go, your body follows." Simply keeping your eyes directly on your man wasn't even close to being enough. Dan had very specific targets for us. Each located at various points on the defender's body that we would isolate and focus on depending on what we were trying to accomplish.

Any given run block would have one of four specific "fits" or "positions" for covering up a different amount of your man depending on where you had to be in relation to the overall play. Sometimes, you had to really work to reach a defender (position 4) because it was a wide outside play. Or maybe the play was coming right up behind you on your inside. In that case, you need to be more "minus" on your man (position 1). The difference in some of these positions was miniscule in measurement, but that difference was critical in terms of play success. Dan would explain a position two block as having your left big toe JUST inside the defender's right big toe. No more, no less. Your face would have your left nostril just to the right of the defender's sternum. No more, no less. Extremely specific. To get to that position required unbelievable focus with your eyes. You needed to learn to lock in that pinpoint spot on the defender's jersey in your stance, then never lose that lock. As you could imagine, the second the ball got snapped, all hell broke loose. You needed to have trained your visual focus to such a level that even amongst the chaos, your eyes stayed glued on target.

Visual Focus Training

"Your eyes take your hands, and your hands take your body, and your body takes your feet," was another one of Dan's highly repeated phrases, and as much as I hated hearing him repeat that every time I missed fitting a position, he was always right. Where your eyes go, so do you. That means, the attention you give to your visual focus is absolutely critical. So, we trained visual focus, and we trained it a lot.

Dan had all kinds of goofy drills for this. He'd come out with this little black dot drawn on the palm of his hand and stand maybe ten feet in front of us, get us in our pass protection stance, and have us track his hand with just our eyes. We were to only respond with any other body movement if he moved any of his body OTHER than the arm with the dot on his hand. Once he had our full attention and focus, he'd start messing with us. He'd run back and forth with that hand out in front, prompting us to react and kick and slide back and forth with him. Then, he'd stop on a dime and start shooting his hand up in the air or firing it out to the side to see if our heads would shoot out along with it. He'd get us from time to time, but as with everything else, with practice, our discipline improved.

I learned to focus, to concentrate on a single target, and to keep that focus throughout the duration of the madness that is a football play. Now, Dan was taking me to graduate school. It was time for Focus 2.0. — learning to stay completely zeroed in on that target while at the same time seeing everything else that was going on around me. In short, I had to learn to be a Jedi.

Spatial Focus

I don't think that's an actual term. I soon came to realize that just as the sport of football seems to have its own language, so does Dan. I played for him for so long that his words and phrases have become normalized in my vocabulary to the point that I just assume they're real. It's not until I get puzzled looks from people that I remember that football lingo isn't naturally understood by most.

"Pay attention!"

Dan could sense my focus wavering. No way would he guess it was drifting to old Rocky scenes, but, nevertheless, I needed that verbal slap in the face.

"Focus – RIGHT HERE!" He pointed again to the I and O on his shirt. I was in my half squat pass protection stance, hands up, ready for action with my eyes glued to those one-inch high letters. Not the L, not the N or the S, and definitely not the whole LIONS word. That would not be focused enough. All good, I had my focus back exactly where it needed to be. Now time for the training.

Learning to "See Both"

Dan was maybe one or two feet in front of me. Close quarters, just like a big defender would be. The I and the O were my visual target for where my hands would go, if and when it was time to engage with a punch. This drill, though, now added a wrinkle. Dan had both his arms stretched way out to the sides, making him look like a scarecrow. His hands were both opened wide. He began randomly altering his hands to make his fingers represent different numbers. Sometimes, his right hand would flash a two then maybe his left would make a four. There was no set pattern. Sometimes, he would flash different numbers from the same hand three times in a row. It was all very random. The objective for me was to call out the numbers he was creating the second he made them. The trick was to never lose my laser lock on the I and O to do it. This was not easy. He was so close to me that I had a very poor natural peripheral angle. Just like Luke Skywalker responding to Yoda, I, too, believed Dan was asking the impossible, but once again, he proved that any skill can be improved with focused practice. That's just what ended up happening. I started to gain spatial focus, to learn as Dan often said "to see both."

This skill is extremely critical in offensive line play. There is so much twisting of defenders and passing off of those twists between us linemen that you need to be able to see it coming. You need to "see through" your defender as Dan would remind us. You need to see both your target and what's happening around it.

> **That ability to see both allows you to proactively deal with changes and adjustments sometimes before they actually happen.**

Spatial focus allows you to stay out in front of what's happening because you don't get buried in just what's in front of you; you also see what's going to be happening next. It's doubly important for my position at center. I had to be able to scan the entire defense to understand what they were up to in order to get everybody blocking the right people while at the same time being locked into my own assignment and whatever specific target this play called for me to attack. That wasn't always easy. Hence the extreme volume of work Dan put into developing that ability.

The Takeaway

Spatial focus, the ability to concentrate completely on the task at hand while never losing sight of everything else that is going on around you, may very well be the most important super-skill for an offensive lineman. Dan trained me to see the forest AND the trees at the same time. To see the small and big picture simultaneously. And he taught me to deal with the three-hundred-pound problem directly in front of me while also processing the rest of the defense's movement happening behind him.

SEEING THE UNSEEABLE

"To be a great center, you need to have eyes in the back of your head."

~ **Dan**

This was going to take a miracle. Our perfect season was on the line. There was just over six minutes left in the game, and we were trailing 15–5. Due to injuries, we were down to our third string quarterback, Buck Pierce. As this point in his career, Buck had played zero snaps. We were on the road, playing the Riders in the most hostile environment that exists for a visiting team in the entire league. It was August 27, 2005. We had entered that game a perfect 8–0. Our team was loaded with so much talent that our backup quarterback Casey Printers was the reigning league's most outstanding player – and he was our back up. But now we had trouble. Both our All-Star quarterbacks were injured. Our hopes of keeping our winning streak alive had come down to Buck and a prayer.

Many great things happened in those final six minutes. We rallied as a team, our All-Stars came through big time, Buck grew up as a pro, and on our eighth final play of that game I grew eyes out of the back of my head.

Sometimes Unsound Football Beats You

We were stuck right around mid-field. With time running out, we needed a big play. We needed to get into scoring position, and fast. As you could imagine, Saskatchewan could smell rookie blood and wanted to end this game right then and there. They were going to send the house at Buck. Back in 2005, we didn't have as many answers in our pass protection world as we do today. If the protection call had me working to the right, our left side had only two linemen to protect that side. They had a built in "squeeze" rule, so that if a third defender was to add in and run through their inside, they would both squeeze down to stop him. This would leave the farthest man to the outside unblocked. The thinking is to always protect the most direct line to the quarterback first. Very sound in principle. What we didn't have back then was an answer if they brought two extra men through the inside gap. There was no "double squeeze" call. Somebody was going to come free and that somebody would be racing right up the middle to destroy our quarterback. We didn't have it in our system because nobody ever brought that many second level players through the same gap. It's unsound football. But on that particular play, that's exactly what Saskatchewan did. They pretty much brought everybody.

My strict rules had me protecting anything that came through the immediate gap to my right. If and when something did, my detailed and heavily trained instructions were to always "double uppercut" that charging defender with my left hand, cupping underneath the chest pad of his right jersey number and doing the same with my right hand under his left jersey number. My eyes were trained to zero in right on the tiny CFL logo stitched between the two sewn on numbers. Very specific and very effective.

Zero Responsibilities to My Left ... But

Sure enough, the second that ball was snapped, they all came charging. I had a linebacker in my face in a "New York Minute" as Dan would always say. That was that for me. With my eyes pierced on his jersey logo, both my hands hit their targets. It was a perfect fit. Right on contact, I hunkered down and squeezed my grip. I had my man locked down. Focused vision does not stop post contact. If anything, it gets magnified. You need to keep your eyes glued to your target throughout the duration of the entire block. "Where your eyes go, so does your body," was Dan's constant saying that always proved true. If you want to stay tightly fitted to your task, you better keep your eyes fixated on your target. Never wander.

For some reason, though, I sensed something. It's hard to have complete clarity of things you cannot see, but my intense spatial focus training had heightened my ability to mind my surroundings without having to directly see them. They had indeed brought an extra safety down the middle. Our left side had already squeezed down to pick up the blitzing linebacker through the middle gap. We didn't have any rules back then for them to squeeze even more to account for an additional late blitzing safety.

> **The speed at which your mind can process information and translate that information into physical action is a direct result of the amount of training it has been given in that environment.**

I may not have seen Dan's hand flashing a two or a four off to my left, but I sure as heck sensed a green jersey coming through. Without breaking focus on my block for even a second, I stuck out my left arm as far as my stumpy limb would extend. It was just enough. My open palm jammed the charging safety in his chest. Instinctively, I shuffled slightly to my left to do all I could to now split the two defenders in half. I only had one hand on each. It may not go down as the prettiest block in my career, but it definitely was effective. I was able to buy Buck enough time to hit our All-Star receiver Jason Clermont over the middle for a huge thirty-two yard gain. That crucial play did three things:

1. It extended our drive that ultimately ended with a touchdown.

2. It stopped Saskatchewan from bringing the house like that on us for the remainder of the game.

3. I invented a new technique that Dan would refer to as the "Take Two" technique from then on.

We went on to win that game in dramatic fashion. Buck became an overnight star, and our winning streak, at least for a few more weeks that season, remained intact.

The Takeaway

Those situations came up time and time again throughout my career. The more Dan kept training my "spatial focus" skill, the more I kept being able to see without ever losing sight of my immediate target. It's something I can now no longer turn off. My wife is maybe the only one that can see it. She can tell that I am giving her my full focus while still processing everything else that is happening in my periphery. To give maximal attention to the task in front of you without ever losing sight of the bigger picture…that's valuable.

ON MAKING DECISIONS – LEARNING HOW TO SELL

"Volume reflects confidence."

~ **Dan**

"How fast is it moving out there, Angus?"

"About 90 mph, coach."

"We need to get that speed down to about 5 mph. And we will, trust me, we will."

This was bad. Wally was now involved, and he was pissed. It's not good when the head coach has to get involved in a team drill. They usually sit back, observe, and let their coaches coach. Mistakes would happen; blocks would be missed, but all would be reviewed and discussed during film. When the issue is preventing the entire practice from moving forward, though, now you have a problem that a head coach can't let continue. Unfortunately for me, I was the problem.

Day Three of Training Camp

Some people call it hump day. The day the body is at its sorest. The last day before adaption starts to kick in, and the body begins to accept this horrible feeling as normal and adjusts accordingly. Or maybe it just goes numb to it all. I never really bothered to figure out exactly how the body handles camp. I do know that in 20+ years of football training camps, the body finally decides to do whatever it does to get you to a place where you stop thinking about your overall soreness and focus on improving your play after day three.

2003 was still the old days. These were real two-a-days. Two full contact practices, day after day after day. It's bananas what we used to do now that I'm removed and have perspective, or maybe I'm just getting old and having trouble remembering what my body used to be capable of. Either way, those camps were hard.

Day three that year was especially challenging for me. Beyond the physical fatigue, the mental strain of learning and directing a brand-new complex blocking scheme was starting to overwhelm my brain. The first two days were fine. Dan did a great job of layering the system from the ground up. Simple, base protections and bread and butter run players were installed first. What made it even easier was that our defense followed the same pattern. Simple, static, base fronts composed almost all of the looks I saw those first two days. Sure, I missed a block here and there, everybody does, but for the most part, I felt in charge. I was seeing things clearly and relaying to my troops how we were going to go about blocking them.

Confidence Can Leave You...Fast

Sometimes, it doesn't take much. Mine took off and hid that afternoon during our first no-huddle, blitz pick-up session of the year. Gone were those nice static fronts the defense had been kind enough to present to me. The friendly confines of an offensive huddle were gone, too. That safe place where you could gather yourself and talk things through between plays. *"No sir,"* as Dan would often say. This was chaos...and my job was to make sense out of it for everyone. I was failing miserably.

All of a sudden, the defense was a blur. There were players moving around all over the place. Just when I thought I might have a handle on what they were doing, they would move again. All this was happening while I was trying to focus on the play call that was getting barked out while we were up at the line. Trying to get your brain to process verbal and visual information simultaneously is not always an easy task. Focus likes to have one purpose. It doesn't respond nicely to being pulled in opposite directions. When circuits get overblown, they short out and shut down. That's what happened to my brain. Things were moving too fast for me to process. My undertrained brain couldn't keep up. Panic set in, and mental paralysis took over. The end result? No action. No blocking call. And worst of all, no ball got snapped.

Dan always had little sayings and phrases to describe what he was seeing on "tape." Some you loved to hear; others were only funny if they weren't referencing you. Playing like a "skilled surgeon" was one of his higher verbal honors. Giving Dan "clinic tape material" gave you the added knowledge that he would probably showcase that play around North America at coaching conferences.

Being "clinic tape material" was big time.

As far as full line group performance went, there was one gold standard you wanted to hear above all else: "That looks like a symphony in motion." Of all the praise Dan would dish out, none topped that. Being a "symphony in motion" or a "masterpiece in precision" meant o-line perfection. I've never heard Dan utter either of those statements without a huge smile on his face.

For every up, there is a down. For every yin, there is a yang. And for every "symphony in motion," there is a "broken accordion." That's one thing you didn't look forward to hearing, especially when you were the broken piece causing the rest of the accordion to fall apart. That's exactly what I was that afternoon drill period, and it sucked.

Hitting Decision-Making Bottom

My inability to allow the play to even begin resulted in the worst-case scenario: Wally pulling me from the drill! When your head coach and general manager is removing you, you have really found yourself on some serious thin ice. That rarely happens. Positional coach pulling you? Sure. The head coach and GM? That meant you were screwing up far beyond hurting just yourself; you were hurting the development of the team. Not a great impression to make on the man that is ultimately responsible for you sticking around or having to look to the classified section for your next form of employment.

As embarrassing as that was for me, I see now how tough it must have been for Dan. He had to have been embarrassed, too. A head coach stepping in and pulling one of his guys is also a reflection on him as a coach. Why was one of his guys not better prepared? And why didn't Dan step in and do something? That's a tough spot for a positional coach to be in. He got evaluated just like I did. His evaluation was based on his ability to prepare his players. Having the head coach make the decision for him couldn't have been an easy pill to swallow. I could see how he might have publicly scolded me if nothing more than to save face by unleashing a visual public displeasure at my ineptness. He didn't. Dan was far too professional to ever fall for those childish, impulsive, reactionary responses.

He came over, looked me in the eye, softened his intense stare, and simply said, "Just relax for a bit. We'll figure this out after." That was it. He didn't throw me back in the fire for the rest of that period. I'm sure that had a lot had to do with the fact that Wally stayed to watch and that may have been viewed as a dangerous power move. I have no idea. I like to think it was because he knew the power of pausing. The power of gaining some distance and slowing the emotions. Not doubling down with more pressure before we resolved the underlining issue. This was a time for me to unplug, to stop the bleeding, to gather myself and do no more harm. We would revisit this issue shortly; generally during post-practice meetings, then specifically following that very meeting. What ended being a 30 minute delay in me getting to team dinner became my one-on-one counseling session on how to make decisions with clarity amongst chaos.

The Bottom Line

"Angus…I need you to know something."

It was just me and him in the room now. The other guys had been dismissed for dinner. I came to learn that when these one-on-one meetings were requested there was a reason, and it was always a good one. Dan never asked someone to stick around and use their own time without something very important to discuss. He wanted that privacy to make sure all focus and attention were given to you and you only. For a second, I thought he might be informing me I was going to be released. Who knows? I wasn't much more than a rookie with no other track record for them to evaluate me on other than the ineptness I had just displayed. He just kept that dead eye lock on me through a pause that seemed to never end. It finally did.

"Nothing can happen until you make a decision. NOTHING."

He really emphasized that second nothing. Not in an angry way, just making sure that I was absolutely clear of the importance of my task: to make a decision.

Every single play I ever ran in my entire 13-year career had at least some kind of blocking call. Some were simple while others were complex, but there has never been and will never be a play that doesn't have at least some verbiage used by us to confirm we all know what to do given the defensive front presented to us.

That's the end decision. That's the one that directs final action. That's the call that gives the group a chance to be a "symphony in motion" or a "masterpiece in precision." Without that call, the group is a symphony without a maestro, a ship without a rudder, an accordion without .... whatever the main piece is that keeps an accordion together. Bottom line? Decisions lead to action. Indecision leads to inaction or at the very least, hesitant, non-confident action. My job was to make that decision and to make it every single time. Sounds easy enough, but when the world in front of you is moving around at speeds your brain can't keep up with, it's hard to know HOW to come up with that final choice.

"It's Moving Fast Out There, Isn't It Angus?"

It was a question he was already answering for me.

"Yeah. It was pretty fast today, coach."

My drop in confidence was reflected in the weak pitch and tone of my response. Dan did what he could physically to keep my defensive wall down. He softened his own tone and greatly relaxed his body posture. This was serious time, and he needed me open and ready to hear, not defensive and closed.

> **"Here's the thing, Angus, it's only going to get faster unless we find a way to slow it down."**

For some reason that statement really scared me. I was doing all I could, but I just couldn't think fast enough to figure out what call to make. If I couldn't do it in day three of camp, what chance would I have come regular season?

"Angus, do you remember in the off-season when we went over the call checklist?"

Again, I knew Dan knew this answer because we had also gone over it four days ago at the start of training camp. He turned the film back on. Somehow, he had the very play I got pulled by Wally from all teed up and ready to go. That was impressive given the fact that we had just finished team meetings and had just been watching that very film, and it wasn't anywhere near that spot. I thought better than to divert the conversation to such trivial curiosities, though.

"Okay, here we go, Angus. You're up at the line. Let's go through this."

Things Are Always Much Clearer When You Watch It on Film

You not only get a completely different vantage point, but you also have all the time in the world to pause the play and sit there and talk it out. Even still, on this particular play, there was too much movement. They refused to set themselves and give me a clear enough picture to make a call with.

"Every picture needs a call, right Angus?"

"Yes, but Dan..."

He stopped me right there.

"The question is, Angus, what tools are you using to get yourself to that final call, that final decision?"

He wanted to make this point really clear.

"Stop trying to guess what the right decision is, just go through the checklist one by one, and don't ever skip a step."

He let the film run now.

"Forget the call right now. First things first. What personnel grouping are they in?"

There were only two options ever available for me to choose from and the decision was predicated on the people they had on the field. No matter where they were lined up or were walking around, they either had three big bodied defensive linemen out there or four. We knew who their big body personnel was from previous film study. It was easy to see if they were on the field or not. That simple first step did two things:

1. It gave me a task to focus on that was always answerable, which helped create focus and enhanced confidence.

2. Once decided, it eliminated at least half of the possible options from my decision-making Rolodex, narrowing my margin for error greatly.

"Well, Angus, what is it? Are there three big bodies out there or four?"

It was overly obvious that they had 4 big bodies on the field.

"Four, Dan."

"No, no," he said. *"The call is – FOUR DOWN!"*

He wanted me to rehearse the checklist properly, always looking to build habits as close to real life as possible.

"Okay. Great. We've established their personnel. Now, you need to decide if it's an even or an odd front."

An even front simply meant that I was uncovered, where an odd front meant they had a big body moved down right over top of me. Sometimes, they wouldn't show this until very late. As I got older, I became much faster at adjusting my calls to reflect any late movement. But for now, Dan just wanted me to make a decision.

"Well, Angus? Is it even or odd?"

"I don't know, Dan. They haven't finished moving yet."

"Let me ask it another way then." He was careful never to match my frustration with his. He stayed calm. *"Right now, is there anybody over you or not? That's all that matters at this point in the checklist progression."*

"No, coach. I'm uncovered."

"Well then?"

He left that question there for me to fill in the appropriate response.

"Even," I said it almost sheepishly, reflecting how embarrassed I was in this moment to not have been able to follow this simple process earlier on the field.

"Okay, then, good. Even it is. I'm with you on that."

With that, Dan didn't even need to say another word. I knew what the call was and softly cut right to the chase – *"LEO 37, 52 OUT."*

Dan's voice boomed right back. *"PERFECT, ANGUS!"* He cracked an approving smile. *"You've been making this way too complicated for yourself. Stop trying to look out there at all that confusion and make a decision based on it. That won't work, and I will also have no way of helping you."* He then leaned in, slowed his voice way back down, and with a deep eye lock gave me some final pre-dinner advice. *"Never ever forget to run through the decision-making checklist. There will be times when you think you already know the answer at first glance, even then, always run through the list."*

It was something that took time to master, to keep clarity of mind amongst all the chaos to stay disciplined to the process. To not skip steps, to follow the rule-based system each and every time. It greatly helped turn down the noise by focusing my attention on an answerable question that always led to another answerable question that almost always resulted in the right decision staring me directly in the face. The checklist brought order to chaos. It made things clear and seeing things clearly for what they really are may be one of the most important things you can ever do when making a critical decision that will greatly affect your ability to succeed or not.

"Angus, before you go, there's something else I want you to know."

We had been going through the checklist of calls for maybe thirty minutes. We ran through 15 or so separate plays, and Dan had me rattle off the personnel I saw, covered or uncovered, and ultimately deliver the final call. We had done enough for the night. His point was not only clear, but we did enough visual and verbal reps in that meeting room that he could clearly see I understood and was able to roll through the process quite well.

Decision-Making 2.0

Now for the quick chat on decision-making 2.0. It was much less a chat and more of a statement. It was a phrase Dan would repeat many times throughout my career, but really, in my case, he never needed to again. He once again stared me dead in the eyes, took that long pause of his, and with a booming voice barked out *"VOLUME REFLECTS CONFIDENCE!"*

Then he stopped. I think he wanted that phrase to really sink in and not have it lost amongst a bunch of other ramblings. *"I want you to think about that tonight, Angus."* Another pause. *"Remember, the men around you are looking to you for what to do. They need to not only believe you but believe in you. Volume reflects confidence, Angus. When you speak out there, you make sure they know you believe in what you're saying. You show them that you have confidence in your call, and they will have confidence in it, too. It's not just a matter of knowing the right call. It's a matter of making sure your teammates believe you. Give them that confidence, Angus. Deliver your call with volume. The type of volume that leaves no question in anybody's mind that you know what you're doing. That you're in charge. People need to feel that. Give it to them every single time."*

The Takeaway

I have never forgotten that chat. Once you learn the checklist process to help get you to the very best decision possible, it's time to sell that decision. To sell it to yourself and the troops around you. Volume reflects confidence. Obviously, proper volume is a relative thing based on whatever situation you may find yourself in. There is no doubt, though, that on a football field, quietly mumbling out your calls will do nothing to help instill that all important buy-in from your teammates in the trenches where trust and confidence reigns above all else. I may not have gotten every call right the rest of my career, but I can tell you I delivered each and every one of them with the level of volume that left no doubt in my teammates mind that I believed in the call we were going with. We could always figure out and correct mistakes; that was the easy part. It would have been much harder to have to figure out and correct a lack of confidence. Solid volume took great care of that every single time.

My Final Sales Lesson: The Speed of Real Life

It was all a blur again. It was as if someone just pressed the fast-forward button on everything and everyone around me and hit pause on my thinking ability at the same time. Once again, I froze.

I didn't even hear the word "hut."

It's amazing how loud your internal noise can become when you lose control of the volume dial. The accordion was once again broken. My line mates all popped out of their stances without a clue what to do. They knew hut meant go, but void of ANY direction whatsoever by me, they each hesitantly fired out with different intentions. The defense responded to their non-unified movement. To the viewer watching from the stands or at home, everything resembled the start of a play. Everything except one crucial thing…the ball never got snapped. I was still stuck there, like a statue in my stance over the ball — my mind too overwhelmed by the extreme defensive movement to make enough sense out of it to come to a decision and ultimately take any action.

It was mid-summer 2004. I had done a pretty good job over the last year and a half of making decisions, relaying them, and selling confidence to both my line mates and sometimes, more importantly, to myself. I hadn't always been right, but as Dan constantly reminded me, *"If everyone is on the same page, we've got a chance."* It was my job to get everyone on that same page, to decide how best to block any given play, and to sell it with both "volume and clarity." Those two very important tid-bits to gain the confidence of those around you. And when you can hardly hear yourself think, volume and clarity can become more than a subtle selling tip; they become a necessity.

The difference between this time and back in training camp was this was a live game. There was no ability to stop the drill. No ability to take some time to get me to cool down or have Dan come out and go over it all with me. No sir! This was the real deal with 35,000 fans paying good money to watch their team compete, not to see a young center forget to even snap the ball.

It was early first quarter, and we were hosting the mighty Montreal Alouettes. We entered that week 2–3, a disappointing start to what was supposed to be a promising season. Montreal was their standard 6–0.

They dominated the late nineties and most of the 2000s. They were a formidable foe whose defense was every bit as good as their high-powered, star-studded offense. Some saw them as unbeatable. Not Dan.

He had studied them relentlessly and had come up with a game plan to exploit them where he felt we could. We were going to run the ball all game on them. Right up the middle. An old school football approach that is rarely seen in the pass happy 3-down world of Canadian football. His straight up the middle plan, however, wasn't going to be your traditional, simple, block the man in front of you and ram it right down their throats. Oh no! He had something special planned.

Going Old School

Dan went deep into his own archives and dug up an old play he used to run when he coached back in the day at the College of the Holy Cross in Worcester, Massachusetts. When I mean archives, I'm serious . We ended up watching Holy Cross practice clips that were in BLACK and WHITE. The play is called WHAM. It has recently made its way back into mainstream football in one form or the other, but in 2004, nobody ran it. We would be catching Montreal completely off guard.

It was a running play to essentially "cut the defense in half" as Dan explained it. Or in even better Dan terms, we would be opening up the defense "like the parting of the Red Sea!" He said that phrase with way more than just a subtle grin. We were simply trapping one of their inside defensive linemen. We would leave him completely unblocked, enticing him to run straight ahead as if we had forgotten about him. Then, one of our fullbacks, or WHAMbacks, would come sprinting diagonally down the line and unexpectedly blindside him. If done right you would send him flying, opening up a HUGE space right up the middle for our ball carrier to gain easy yards before ever even coming into contact with anybody.

Dan LOVED this play. I have never again seen him more excited about any play we specifically added in for an opponent at any other time during the remainder of my career. He was like a kid that was holding the answer to a test nobody thought we could pass. He was giddy and confident. WHAM would work. There was only one issue: the play and how it was executed varied greatly depending on the defensive look. There were multiple options for who we would choose to WHAM. Our WHAM blocker needed to know who we were leaving for him to block just as much as we did. Everything depended on me. I had to orchestrate Dan's magic. The decision of who to WHAM wasn't a hard one on the chalk board, or even that week during practice. Players lined up where we wanted them to, and I made the call based on given parameters. Easy.

The Difference Between Theory and Reality

There was a reason Montreal was 6–0, though. They were great at NOT making things easy for you when you actually got on the field against them. It seems they had a defensive game plan adjustment for us as well. For the first time that season, they changed from being a static front to a continuous movement front. They didn't just line up in their stance and say, "This is where we are – go ahead, Angus, make your decision." That would have been far too kind of them. Oh no! They had decided to be a defense that didn't settle into position at all! They never stayed put. Everyone kept in constant motion, making it nearly impossible to choose one of the many pictures I had studied leading up to this game. Nothing was how we rep'd it. I was lost.

Sometimes Things Don't Go According to Plan

This was our first attempt at the play, and it was a disaster. My inability to make a call or even snap the ball not only cost us a five-yard penalty, but much worse, it exposed our secret plan without having the benefit of even getting to use it.

We couldn't go back to it. Not now anyway. It was 1ˢᵗ and 15, and I was far too rattled to rely on to make the right decision. We reverted to basic offense. Two and out is never a great response to a 1ˢᵗ down penalty, but that's just what we did. I came off fuming. I think showing anger in football is an instinctual response to embarrassment.

> **You show anger as the manly mask to hide frustration. It never works. In fact, it just gets in the way of being in the right frame of mind to deal with the issue, fix it, and move forward.**

Cooler Heads Always Prevail

Dan always knew exactly how to regain our focus. There was no anger, no rage, no adding gas to my self-built, non-helpful fire. There was a calming pause and a simple, direct, information-gathering question.

"Angus, on the WHAM call, what personnel grouping were they in?"

Looking back now, I'm one hundred percent sure he already knew the answer. I also now realize that he was one hundred percent certain that I didn't. He wasn't asking a question so much as making a statement to prove a point. He did it in such a way, though, that I didn't take it as such. I only heard a sincere question. That removed any need for an ego protecting confrontational response by me. I really thought he was hoping I could enlighten him with my answer. A simple question can direct focus. You are where you place your focus; therefore, the quality of questions asked can help dictate the quality of your actions as a result of the direction of your focus. My answer was embarrassing but one he already knew.

"I don't know, Dan. They were all moving around so much. It was a blur."

His response was dramatic in its power, *"Okay...it's okay."* That short, simple, calming statement went miles toward my opening up to everything he would say next.

A Quick Refresher in Decision-Making

Dan went into a very precise, cheat sheet version of the rules for decision-making that he had outlined for me so long ago. He only had about 60 seconds, so each word had to matter. Time is precious, even more so during a game. This little talk had to accomplish two things:

1. Remind me of the rules of decision-making

2. Give me the confidence necessary to stick to them

He blended those two objectives into one short lecture.

"Angus, I need you to hear me now. We need you to make a decision. I don't give a damn how much they are moving out there. They either have three down personnel out there or four. You can figure that out, right?"

"Yes, Dan."

He stared directly at me and said, *"I need to make sure we are in clear agreement on that?"* His eyes were now piercing through me. *"You can always tell if they are in three down or four down personnel, right?"* He wanted a much more confident response than I had just given him.

"YES!" I shouted back with the same volume he demanded of me out there on the field.

"Good." He seemed confident in my confidence on that. *"Now, if you call three down, then you know someone will end up over you; you can guarantee that fact. The question is, will they also cover the guards. It's either an ODD call if the guards are uncovered, or an ACE CHECK STRONG call if they are. That's it; one of two choices."* He was borderline shouting but still able to maintain complete clarity and control of his voice. *"Same as with a FOUR DOWN call. You now know you won't be covered. You now only have to make one of two choices: a YOU or ME call. Base that decision on who you think has better leverage but know either one CAN work."*

Dan really had a way of explaining what seemed complex and making me realize how simple it actually was. **It was a matter of not skipping crucial steps in the decision-making process, running through the checklist properly every single time, not mentally skipping to the end and just making a decision based on nothing more than feel and hope, committing to the steps.**

"Look at me, Angus." He now wanted to cement that information by instilling confidence in me to take charge. *"I will tell you again — we can't run a play unless you make a call. We need you to lead us out there. As long as you can come off the field each and every time and tell me what personnel they are in, I'm with you on whatever call you make – 100%. I'm in. As long as you decipher what personnel they are in each and every time, I promise you, whatever call you make will be the one we will win with."*

The Takeaway

Wow! I can't tell you what that did for me. He reminded me of the importance of not skipping steps in the decision-making process and then empowered me to choose what I thought best to do with 100% backing from him. That's powerful stuff right there. When things are going crazy all around you, the very last thing you need is more craziness from your coach. What you need is calmness, clarity, and confidence. Dan supplied all three of those in bucket loads, not just that night, but for the course of my entire career. I ran back on the field fixated on one thing and one thing only – determining what personnel they had on the field. Everything else was nonsense noise. That singular purpose cut through all the chaos, sharpened my focus, and kicked the decision-making checklist into gear. From there, the decisions became almost obvious.

BONUS YARDS: ELIMINATE AND CONQUER

After that, it became easy. They could move around all they wanted. I was focused on only one thing: did they have three big bodies on the field or four? That's it. That's all I was concerned with. No amount of movement could hide that reality. Found them– "FOUR DOWN!" I screamed at the top of my lungs, leaving absolutely no doubt in anyone's mind. I just cut half the confusion out right there. Was anybody over me or not? Just look in front of me. Nope. "EVEN!" Just narrowed the choices down a ton more. Only one decision left to make: the "YOU" or "ME" call. In the end, either one would work. Screw it. "ME!" I shouted with so much volume and clarity that my parents probably heard it from mid-way up section 45. Wow! That not only felt great, but it worked. I got the call out, no problem, and relayed it to everyone with the type of volume and clarity that left them no doubt about what we were doing and that it was going to work. Dan's brilliant strategizing could finally take shape. And boy did it ever! We ran that WHAM play all night on them. The more they kept trying to confuse us with different looks, the better the play kept working. I stayed true to my promise to Dan. All I cared about was finding the personnel, choosing ODD or even FRONT, then making my decision. Using that simple deductive checklist every single time. I can't tell you how much clarity that brought to the previous confusion I saw. Trying to jump right to the final call without taking the appropriate steps to get to that place was nothing more than guessing and hoping. Neither are suggested strategies; they're an absence of one. What works and works every time is a system. In a confusing world, a deductive system works like a charm. A simple checklist gives you easy choices to start with that help remove most of the noise, narrowing down the options, and usually resulting in a much cleaner picture from which to make a final choice.

We went on to dominate Montreal that night. Dan's WHAM play left them clueless, which resulted in a group of hesitant defenders, and that made them easy prey. We ran the ball 24 times for 120 yards. WHAM was every bit as effective as Dan had predicted. All it needed was for me to make a call. That little sideline reboot was exactly what I needed for the rest of the night. I ended up playing my very best game of that entire season. I played so dominantly, in fact, that I ended up being honored as the CFL's lineman of the week. It was an amazing accomplishment considering how that game began for me. It was also an honor I would never achieve again. That game also set in motion a confidence in me that carried forward. I finished that season not only as a first time All-Star, but also ended up being our team's nominee for the league's Outstanding Lineman of the Year award. I never again missed making a call. They weren't always the right ones, but I always had my reasons, and they were based on the deductive checklist. With that system in place, it made it very easy for Dan to help me work through my incorrect calls and see where my misunderstanding took place.

That game changed a ton of things for me and my career. Things very easily could have gone the other way. I was mentally shaken when I came off the field after that first WHAM disaster. I wasn't really sure if I could figure any of this out. When the enemy smells fear, they tend to go for the kill. If Dan hadn't masterfully reset my mind and confidence levels, I cringe to think how bad that night may have gone…along with maybe the rest of my career.

LEARNING HOW TO LEARN – PART 2

ON ENGRAINING A SKILL

"The comforting edge is you can beat people with technique."

~ **Dan**

"CUP!" I screamed at the top of my lungs. If volume did indeed reflect confidence, I was making damn sure I sounded like the most confident man on the field. On this particular play, I actually was. It was a few days later in camp, and we were right in the thick of the afternoon's inside run period, a daily part of practice where all we do is our bread and butter run plays. Like most specialized drill periods, the offense loses the distinct advantage of surprise. The defense ALWAYS knows we are running the ball. That can make things somewhat tougher.

We were running a counter play. Counters were great against certain defensive schemes, in particular, defenses that aligned players in the gaps between offensive linemen (as opposed to right in front of them). It allowed us to take advantage of those natural leverage angles and split the defense open at our chosen point of attack. On this particular down, we were running a counter play to the left – "South Leopard." All of our counter plays were coded as various safari cats. Why? I have no idea. That was always way above my pay grade. The "SOUTH," or any other cardinal direction put in front, alerted us that the play was going left. Why? Because that's what we did. It was simple, and it worked, good enough reason for me. The left side of the line would all block the players to their right, or inside. Ideally, caving them backside away from the play. We would pull two of our linemen from the backside. The first would drive out the lone front side unblocked defender, while the second would turn up through the now massive hole created by those other blocks.

In a perfect world, the running back follows the escort of the second lineman through the hole and then, as Dan would always say, *"It's Katie out the door!"* What that actually means, I have no idea, but in our world, it meant big yards were to be gained.

The backside tackle was always the second puller. Who would be the first puller was a decision left to me. That decision was predicated on what I saw in front of me.

Blocking Schemes in Practice

Blocking schemes in football are designed just like schemes in life: to maximize leverage. If I had a player to my right gap, I would make a "YOU" call to the right guard, prompting him to pull left because I had the better leverage to back block that player. If I had a player to my left gap, then the left guard would have better leverage to back block him, and I would scream "CUP," alerting everyone that I would be pulling, and both guards would be staying in. "CUP" was nothing more than a one syllable word compressing a very descriptive meaning – CENTER U PULL. Most of our code was just that, a compression of phrases pushed into a single syllable call. Dan loved single syllable calls. You could bark them louder; there was less room for misinterpretation, and, as Dan would always say, "they sounded strong."

CUP it was. As I had been instructed, I made the decision, and I made it loud and clear. I was to be the first puller. That meant I had to deliver the kick out block. Of the blocks a lineman has to make for all the various plays there are, the kick out block may be the most violent, especially if you have a defender that sees it coming and decides to attack you. It can be, in Dan's words, a true "car accident." I'd open up and take a six or seven-yard straight line run at a defender, who may choose to hunker down and explode back into me. It ends up looking like two rams launching into each other — both trying to do all they can to knock the other back where he came from. You have two ways of being successful here:

1. Be massively bigger than the other player and simply throw more weight and force at him than his body can handle.

2. Execute perfect form with great leverage on contact.

Option one has never been in the cards for me. Perfect form and execution were my only hopes. This block was classic Crowther. It was a forearm blow technique all the way. I had learned, rehearsed, and mastered it so many times on that unforgiving sled that I could now do it in my sleep. Except this wasn't a sled. This was a two-hundred and eighty-pound man with muscles on his muscles, who was all coiled up and ready to explode back into me.

My Training Served Me Well

Each part of that engrained block flowed seamlessly. It felt natural and smooth. This was the first time I had ever done it live the way Dan had taught it. The first time all of Dan's countless piece by piece building of this block would be properly tested. It worked like a charm. I hit the defender just right. Just in that exact sweet spot I had been not only instructed to hit on the Crowther pad, but had mercilessly repeated again and again. I drove him out a solid five or so yards, giving our backside tackle and running back a hole big enough to bring their whole family through. It was a great play. It felt good to deliver a solid kickout block. A block that, given my undersized stature, was maybe the hardest for me to ever dominate.

It's what happened next that cemented this play in my memory. As I began to head back to the huddle, I saw a streaking blur out of the right side of my eye. My spatial focus training may have still been in its early stages, but this blur was moving at speeds that warranted my attention. It was Dan. He was sprinting as if he was running the ball to daylight again for his alma mater Kent State University. They may be known as the Golden Flashes, but on this day, wearing BC Lions gear, he was more of an orange bullet. He was charging right at me and sporting an intense scowl that made me question everything I thought had just happened. He got right up in my face — I mean inches from my face mask — and just stared. He held that intense stare for what seemed to be an eternity. I had no idea what I could have possibly done so wrong, then with his index finger raised and pointed right at me he finally spoke.

"Angus, if you play with fundamentals and leverage like that, there is NOBODY in this league you can't block! NOBODY!"

That last "nobody" was shouted with the same volume and intensity he demanded of me when making my blocking calls. I had never seen Dan that fired up before, not in the middle of a team drill, at least. I came to realize something about Dan: He almost always only brought the thunder and lightning out for positive comments. If it was great, he went bananas to emphasize and reinforce what you just did. When things were not going well, he always seemed to keep the volume down, always conscious that you probably had enough negative noise blowing up your internal speaker already.

Timing Is Everything, Especially When Praising

That fired up phrase from Dan stayed with me and helped carry me through the rest of my career. It was no secret that I was at a physical disadvantage when it came to my competition. For me to be successful required great attention to the details of my technique. That's what I could do and would have to do. The comforting thing that Dan reminded me that day was that would be enough. Playing with great attention to what you were doing and how you were doing it allowed you to beat just about anybody. It wasn't just what you did, but how well you did it that made the difference. There was only one way to ensure being able to always do that at high speeds with mass confusion all around you — practice. Again and again and again.

Skill Learning Versus Conditioning

Just like when I mastered any other segment of any other skill, Dan would finish on that rep with his all too familiar, *"Bottle that one up and put a cap on it."* He always wanted me to end on a great rep. He knew both the psychological and physical benefit of finishing on one's very best effort. The last rep is the one that stays with you; it's where you pick up from next time. Once you've done it perfectly, stop there bottle it up, put a cap on it and save it for next time. He never wanted us to regress. Never wanted our technique to get sloppy from repetition just for repetition's sake.

The point was to learn a skill, not to build toughness or endurance – that's what the box and all his other crazy workouts were for. Skill building was about detail. It was about getting to that perfect movement and stopping, so you could come back to it again next time. Then, when you've done it just right again, stop again. Slowly, the body recognizes that perfect motion and learns to adapt to that as being how it should always do it. It was painfully slow sometimes getting to that place of great technique, but once there, you did yourself a disservice by over- repping it to the point of compromising form due to fatigue. It was a fine line, one that Dan walked very cautiously. Conditioning was one thing; learning perfect form was another. One, he pushed my physical limits with; the other, he did everything he could to avoid exhaustion.

Engrained Skills Are There When You Need Then

It wasn't working. I simply couldn't get the middle linebacker. This was becoming very frustrating for not only me but our entire offense. It was late summer 2009. We were smack dead in the middle of our day two prep practice for Montreal. The Alouettes were coming to town and boasting yet again another impressive 7–1 record.

After five consecutive years playing in the Western Conference Finals, the wheels were starting to come off our team. We were 3–5 and not the intimidating Lions we had recently become accustomed to being. We'd lost a good chunk of our veterans to free agency and retirement. We were young. We were inexperienced, and we were struggling.

Day two is the work day. It's the day you practice at the closest intensity and environment possible in preparation for the upcoming game. Football is such a physically demanding sport that it can really only be played about once a week. There are usually three structured practices in that window. Day one is a heavy teaching day. The tempo is moderate with a strong emphasis on getting the game plan introduced and understood. Day two is when the dial gets cranked up, and we see how that plan looks at the fullest speed possible. On day three, you dial the intensity back down, clean up any issues lingering from the day before, and work on special situations that may come up. Then it's the day before. That's a physically easy walk-through — a non-contact final dress rehearsal before the pads get strapped on tight, and the final verdict on the quality of your weekly preparation gets made.

Each week a brand-new game plan is created. That plan has to be introduced, learned, understood, practiced, and ideally mastered. Our on-field work is held to no more than two hours a day. That includes warmups, individual technique sessions, and all special teams' work. That doesn't leave a ton of time to physically master the weekly game plan and get the volume of reps in that are needed for all 12 guys to feel confident in each other executing it flawlessly. With that time constraint, not only does every practice matter, but every single repetition you do in practice counts. You can't afford to waste any of them, but that's exactly what we ended up doing. Wasting not just that day two run session, but the day before as well, learning it, and all the time before that by Dan preparing it. It simply wasn't going to work.

Time for a New Approach

For the last four years we had become primarily a wide zone running team. The wide zone is very simple in concept. You want to stretch the defense horizontally. Get them running laterally. As an offensive line, we would open up out of our stance and take off running on a predetermined angle — one that would allow us to reach the defender to our outside. Wide zone right, open up, and run right. Very simple. The genius was that if we stayed true to our visual targets and disciplined on the angle that we ran on, we could never be wrong. We forced the defense to make a decision, and we had an appropriate answer no matter how they chose to respond.

Our philosophy was always the same: all five of us would take off in unison and run to the call side. The back-side guard and tackle would open up a little deeper to get a better angle to do whatever it takes to cut off the two defenders to their right. If done perfectly, they would cut those players down and get them on the ground. The front side of the line, which was me and the play side guard and tackle, would simply run as hard as we could on the same angle and see what the defenders to our right did. If they didn't run with us, we would simply reach them, and off our running back would go around the wide corner untouched. If they ran with us, as most were taught to, we would simply shove them out the way they were running. With the back side cut down and the front side launched out, there was a HUGE gap up the middle for our running back to turn up and run wild. If our back side got their two players cut down, we couldn't lose. For years, it was a thing of magic for us. We chewed up huge chunks of yardage with one simple play. Like Mr. Miagi said in the original and still best *"Karate Kid"* movie – *"If done right, no can defend."*

When Your Opponent Uses Your Rules Against You

Well, it looked like Montreal had found a way to use our own rules against us. A way to make what used to be easy, suddenly impossible.

Our running back had one rule on wide zone: on his third step after the handoff, he had to make a choice. If our play side tackle's head was outside of the defender's, then he was deemed reached. That meant one thing only – keep running like the wind to the outside. If the defender's head stayed outside of our tackle's and refused to be reached, the running back was to turn and run up inside the tackle. The back side would be getting cut off; the hole was up the middle. Simple rules that never failed. Until now.

Jason Jimenez, our monster right tackle, had absolutely no problem reaching Montreal's defensive end. Sure, this was only practice, and our guys were doing the demos, but Dan's ruthless film prep had assured us that this would be the case on game day as well. Perfect. The wide zone would get to the outside every time. The problem was how they coached their middle linebacker, Shea Emery. Usually, middle linebackers flow in response to the movement and angles that we show them. They have responsibilities for their area and that is a fluid space that stays consistent with our movement.

Not these guys. The second our first steps showed wide zone angles, Shea was coached to simply take off and run as hard as he could to the corner, as if sprinting off to the sidelines. This caused a huge issue for us. This wasn't an elaborate multiple player scheme where the end would spike in and the linebacker would loop around; we had answers for that. This was just big Jason reaching the front side defensive end every single time. That domination triggered our back to keep running to the outside. Only now, instead of open field, there was Shea Emery. (Well, during practice, our scout team player representing Shea) right there, completely unblocked, ready to destroy our play for no gain. Shea was my assignment. Getting the middle linebacker on wide zone was one of the things I had really become proficient at; it may have been one of my best abilities.) I had mastered the angles and techniques it took to get most linebackers. For years, hearing a wide zone run call brought a smirk to my face. It was a play I loved to run. It was a play that always made me look good. Now, it just made me the guy whose blocking assignment was destroying our game plan. As a 9-year veteran, this was an infuriating spot to be in. I simply could not get him.

Because of the tight time constraints of practice, we had to move on. The next period was calling. There's never any time during practice to sit around and discuss. That review, discussion, and adaption happens with the coaches during ALL the other hours of the day. There's a reason Dan doesn't have any hobbies. Football doesn't allow time for any of that nonsense.

I went home that night with little confidence in our ability to run the ball against Montreal that week. If we couldn't gain yardage against our scout team, how would we do it against a real defense, especially a top-rated one that knew our M.O. and had a great system for defeating it? They had an answer. What was our response going to be? What could it be?

"Angus, we have a problem."

Dan found me in the weight room early the next morning. When he made that statement, I already knew what the problem was.

"Angus...sorry to interrupt. Let me know when you have a few minutes to chat before meetings." Dan would only ask for our time if it was really important.

"Of course, coach. I'm free right now. What's up?"

"Let's go to the meeting room for a sec, okay?"

This was obviously going to be more than a one-line comment. He had something important to discuss.

"Coach, I know. We can't get the middle linebacker. I've been racking my brain all night. I think I can flatten my angle even more."

"That won't work," he responded. *"He runs too flat. You'll never get him on our zone track."*

Wide zone is what we ran; it was 90 percent of our run game. Without it, we didn't really have a run game. Without one against this Montreal defense, our chances of winning were, as Dan would say, *"Slim to none, and Slim just left town."* What were we going to do?

As a player, I was so fortunate that Dan didn't have any hobbies. Every second of his life was spent solving our problems — searching, researching, dissecting, and finally coming to conclusions based on that work that would give us the very best chance for success.

The Man Had a Plan

"Angus, let me tell you something."

He leaned in and gave me a deep stare with his usual intensity wrapped in a glow of a man excited to share a secret — a secret that only he knew and would share with me, not only alleviating my inability to do my job, but in his view at least, would showcase me in grand fashion.

"We're going to run wide zone. We're going to run it all day on them. We're gonna run it right up their ass!"

The intensity in his face and words grew. It was like watching a volcano build to eruption. Dan wasn't the slightest bit worried about yesterday's performance. He was fired up.

"We're gonna make you a star, Angus!"

Now, he had me really worried. What the heck was he talking about? I couldn't make that block. I had tried every angle possible, and none of them got me there. Why was he so excited?

"We're gonna keep everything the same."

He calmed his voice right back down and slowed his pace. He was almost whispering now. Listening to Dan sometimes was like being on a roller coaster. The tempo and speed went up and then down, fast then slow. It grabbed you and forced you to hold on and pay attention. He was a master at voice variation and impossible not to pay attention to.

"Angus, both you and I know this play is an outside read for our running back all day long, so that's where this play has to go."

"Yes, but Dan…" He stopped me right there.

"Everything will stay the same — except we're going to have you open and pull around. Get you running out in front of our back. Get you out in front to escort our back around the outside. You'll have a nice 10-yard running start to meet Emery at the corner and light…him…up!"

Those last few words were said with a sharp increase in volume and a distinct pause between each. He wasn't just solving the issue Montreal was presenting us; he wanted to shove it right back down their throat. Wow! I didn't know what to think. He made it all sound so easy. Like most things in life, in theory it was; it's actually doing it that can be tricky.

The problem wasn't the concept. It made perfect sense. The issue was that I hadn't really opened up and arc pulled my entire career.

"Dan…you want ME to pull all game? But…"

He stopped me right there. With a dead eye lock and a stare that somehow poured confidence into his next words.

"Just like you've been doing your whole career, Angus. Watch."

He motioned to the screen. He already had some practice film paused and ready to go. I hadn't even noticed it when I walked in because he ALWAYS had practice film cued up and ready to go.

"See that guy? He looks pretty sweet, doesn't he? Looks like a guy that knows what he's doing out there."

He had multiple practice film cut ups of me arc pulling from various technique sessions over the last year or so all strung together. Two things immediately popped into my head:

1. He filmed ALL of my technique session work?

2. When did he have time last night to dig them all up and put this together? Did this man EVER sleep?

Dan quickly steered my attention back to what mattered.

"You see, Angus. You CAN pull. You've been doing it for years. Now, we're just going to let the world know about it."

He concluded that statement with a long pause and a confidence boosting smile. I have no idea the level of confidence he really had in this, but what mattered was the confidence he instilled in me to go out there and actually do it.

Evidence Equals Fact

Showing me that film was important. It reminded me that this wasn't a plan based on hope. Hope is not a strategy. In fact, it is the absence of strategy. Hope is something Dan would never stand for. This decision was based on evidence. Evidence that I not only could do what they were going to ask me to do but had already done at game tempo weekly for years. It was engrained in me, even if it had never been called upon to be used. He didn't show one bit of concern with this plan.

We must have watched maybe 15 or 20 clips. They were a compilation of various arcing pull blocks I had done over the years. Even though they weren't game clips, the speed, intensity, and game-like conditions that Dan made us rehearse in gave me the visual to prove his point. I could pull. I HAD been pulling my whole career.

Dan believed that fundamental blocks are fundamental. Every lineman should not only be taught and helped to master the exact technique of each, but that newly learned skill should be rehearsed and practiced. Not just here and there, and not just any type of practice either. With Dan, there were two things that mattered above all else when looking to engrain, retain, and improve a skill:

1. **Focus**

2. **Frequency**

How frequently could you give full focus to that skill? That's what really mattered. Once Dan had helped us master a movement, he expected us to do it in game-like fashion every time. "Casualness," as Dan would scuff, is the death of mastery. Every time you practiced a skill, you were reminding your body of how you wanted it to work. That is why Dan was so adamant that once we had perfected mechanics, angles, etc., it had been as close to perfect as we could possibly muster. That takes focus. That takes a coach never letting you get lazy or careless with your actions. That took Dan.

Focus – *"That's too damn casual!"* – Dan

We didn't have "walk-through" period; we had "group-teach." It was the same in concept, just very different in mindset. Walk-through suggested just that – walking through your plays against either air or maybe a bag or player simply standing there representing your block. *"Bullshit to that!"* Every single thing we did had to emulate game-like tempo and movement quality. Remember, you are either getting better, or you are getting worse. We don't ever stay the same. Your daily actions dictate which way you go. Are they done at a level and focus that improves what you are trying to improve, or not? You become not just what you repeatedly do, but HOW you do it. Every single rep, no matter if it was pre-practice, individual period, team session, full pads or no pads, needed to be done at game-like speeds with game-like intensity and game like focus. Dan was uncompromising about that. As annoying as it was to never be allowed to "casually" do anything, the payoff as I was about to learn was well worth it.

BONUS YARDS — PULLING

In the case of pulling, my attention process went something like this. After running through my checklist and calling out how we were going to block the front, I would zero in on my man. My visual target for an arc pull would almost always be a front side position three target. My eyes were on the outside edge of his play side jersey number on his chest (even our blocking bags had target dots on them to ensure our visual focus went exactly where it was supposed to). From there, in my stance, I would butt shift away from my pull. (If I was pulling right, I would butt shift left.) This would load the appropriate leg, pre-snap, that I would be using to launch out of my stance. The butt shift is subtle, hopefully not even visibly noticeable. It is extremely important, though, to maximize post-snap efficiency. You need to load that leg correctly so as the ball begins to be snapped, you are already activated to go.

The millisecond the ball begins to move to start the play, it's cave the left knee in. This sinks the ball and big toe of the left foot deep into the ground, maximizing force with which to propel my body to the right. The angle with which you open up your right leg is hugely important. That decision is based on knowing the path of the play and also measuring the movement skills of your target. Both require study and focus. As you push off and open to run, you need to do three things:

1. Get and stay on the correct arc path. This path must be run **perfectly** or you, and ultimately the play, will have no chance.

2. Run with your shoulders out over your knees. This is very important to:

   a. Keep your center of gravity out in front of you

   b. Keep your center of gravity as low as possible, readying you for contact at any time.

3. Keep your eyes directly on your target while maintaining enough spatial focus to not run into other "garbage" that may have come in your way.

Once your arc path, or the defender himself, causes you to turn up field, you need to dip your inside shoulder hard to make that turn. This lowers you even more and allows you to turn up tightly and not end up drifting too wide because of poor pulling mechanics.

This all happens in about 3–4 seconds. It seems like a ton of little details required in such a short period of time, and it is, but that is what's required for success. Each and every one of those steps were taught by Dan piece by piece. Each piece was broken out, explained, rehearsed, and physically mastered before they were put back together into a unified movement. Every single opportunity you had to rehearse that complete block had to be done with full focus and attention to each of those steps. This was vital to not waste an opportunity to ingrain the skill deeper, but to also avoid skill regression through lazy, "casual" movement patterns. Once learned, you had to do it right every single time.

Frequency

Dan loved drills. LOVED them. Any opportunity to specifically hone a skill without the mental distraction of an actual game was special. That was where full focus could be given to mastery, so the movement could be ready for reality. As much as he loved drills, we really didn't have that many. We had a core group of maybe three or four for run blocking and maybe 3–4 for pass blocking. That core group varied only slightly throughout my career. Even then, it was just a tinker here or there. **Fundamental movements are fundamental for a reason. You**

don't need many, but you need to be able to do them well. You also need to do them often.

Dan Gable, legendary wrestler and one of sports' all-time great competitors famously said, *"If it's important to you, do it every single day."* That's solid advice. While we may not have rep'd every single block every single day, it sure seemed like we did. Dan would make sure a week wouldn't go by that we didn't do at least one rep of each block. He knew the importance of Dan Gable's statement, the importance of rehearsal frequency. Even if those blocks had nothing to do with that week's game plan (the way arc pulling had nothing to do with what I normally did), they were still fundamental movements. Fundamental things need to be practiced and practiced often. It's the volume at any given time that becomes less important. Sometimes, we would simply do the blocking movement once. If it was done great, Dan would pull the plug there with his all too familiar command of, *"Bottle that one up and put a cap on it."* We did just enough to keep ingraining perfect motions, that's it. Never pushing to the point of movement breakdown due to fatigue. I learned a very powerful lesson regarding frequency over those years:

1. Keep macro frequency high – practice the skill often
2. Keep micro frequency low – keep the volume very low each training session

Quality over quantity reigns supreme on skill rehearsal for any given session. The real question is, how often can you repeat that fully engaged, full focused work? Do it as often as possible, but do just enough each time to get as close to perfection as possible. Bottle that one up and put a cap on it, then stop, rinse and repeat tomorrow. It doesn't sound sexy, but it works, and I was about to prove Dan's belief in how well it works, even if I wasn't one hundred percent convinced.

Theory Becomes Reality

"Of course, it's working," Dan barked at me with an anger he didn't usually show on the sidelines during games. It was his response to my sprinting off the field shouting at him, *"Dan, it's really working!"* His anger was not at me questioning his belief in what we were doing; it was

more at me questioning the belief in myself to be able to do what he already knew I could.

It was mid-second quarter of that Montreal game. Dan's plan to have me pull on wide zone wasn't just working, it was unstoppable. His adjusted game plan, revealed to me only 48 hours or so hours earlier, was taking shape. Our wide zone was working just as Dan knew it would. Big Jason Jiminez was reaching their defensive end every single time as planned. Their middle linebacker, Shea Emry, raised for the corner every single time as planned. The only thing different was I was now arc pulling to get him every single time. And it was working! I was getting Shea every single time.

It really was a thing of beauty. Anybody watching the game that night would have thought we had been running wide zone that way for years. When in reality, we maybe had three or four repetitions of me pulling during the play, and even those were in a day three non-contact padded environment. It wasn't magic, though, as Dan had reminded me during that morning chat while watching all those film cut ups. I had been arc pulling for years. A rep or two every week over the course of a year or two adds up to a ton of highly focused pulls. That's a lot of highly focused, skill-based practice. It was already ingrained in me. I just never really knew it because I had never been called upon to showcase it. Now, I was, and it was already there for me, built over time.

We had 23 called run plays that day. That's quite a few for the pass happy three down league of Canadian football. We must have run wide zone 19 times. That's a ridiculously high percentage for one play. To make it even more outrageous, I think we ran almost every single one of those wide zones to the right. It got to the point where everybody in the stadium knew what we were doing, but Montreal simply could not stop it. I ended up arc pulling more in that game than the rest of all the plays I had over the course of my entire thirteen years combined.

Our rookie running back, Martell Mallet, ended up rushing the ball 21 times for 213 yards that night, setting a club record and cementing him as the CFL's Rookie of the Year. We blew the doors off Montreal that night.

<u>The Takeaway</u>

That game revealed three key things:

1. We *could* run wide zone on Montreal, and we ran it "right up their ass!" as Dan would love to say with an intense grin.

2. I *could* pull, not because Dan wanted or needed me to, but because he had taught me that skill, and I had been frequently rehearsing it at game speeds and focus continually for years. It wasn't a statement based on hope; it was a statement backed with the confidence of evidence and work.

3. He was going to make me a star. That play showcased me as the lead block out in front of Martell all night. We ran it so many times and were so successful that I was acknowledged after the game as the television broadcasts' "Friday Night Gladiator" – a national award presented weekly to the player who dominated that night's game. It was a great thrill to have the TV crew in the locker room, awarding me a nice limited-edition Movado watch. Such public honors are rare for offensive linemen. I learned to never expect them, making that night all the more memorable.

That game was powerful evidence of the importance of making sure your fundamentals are not just mastered but rehearsed as often as possible with the focus and intensity that matches the real-world requirements of that skill. It was a lesson on constant preparation. The importance of focus and frequency in regards to keeping your skills sharp and keeping them ever ready if and when they may be called upon.

Fundamentals are fundamental for a reason. Don't avoid some because you don't think they're needed for you or you simply don't enjoy doing them. Learn them all. Take the time to master them, then rehearse them as often as possible with full focus and attention to every detail. You can sleep well at night knowing that if that day ever comes when life calls you in for an early morning meeting demanding that skill be put into action, you will be ready to answer the call.

Dan taught me to never rely on hope. That's a fool's game plan. He had us practice, and practice often. He demanded full focus with each rehearsal and emphasized the importance and power of daily, deliberate, focused practice can have on building the type of confidence that comes from evidence-based knowledge of what you can do, because you have already been doing it all along.

ON EVALUATING

"What gets measured gets improved"

~ Dan

Pancakes…linemen are always talking about pancakes. I'm not just referring to breakfast either. I'm talking about the widely used term to acknowledge a block where you literally drive someone off their feet and plant them on the ground flat on their back. Adding insult to injury, the blocker then usually body splashes on top of the humiliated defender further flattening him into a metaphoric human pancake.

As much as that word has become accepted football lingo worldwide, never once had I ever heard Dan utter it. He never used the phrase; in fact, I'm pretty certain Dan may never have even eaten a pancake. He's more a fruit for breakfast kind of guy. We always got rookies to bring doughnuts to meetings for our day before practice. Sometimes, if we were really lucky, a "Rock Star" rookie would show up with a few bags of Egg McMuffins. Just treats to enjoy during meetings on our last work day before the lights get bright and the test becomes real. We offered Dan a doughnut each and every time, but his classic response remained consistent, *"No, thank you! I don't eat those fat pills!"* We did get him to finally take a bite of an Egg McMuffin once and received a, "Not bad." He even flashed an approving grin, before handing the remainder back to me to finish, then straight back to working the film.

Pancakes and pancake literature were just not part of Dan's world, but evaluating and tracking what and how we did things in meticulous fashion was. He tracked and categorized everything. Every single play I had in my entire career with him is accounted for. It had been not only graded, but sub categorized into one of many carefully selected phrases used to decipher what we did and how we did it.

The Power of Clarity

Dan always understood the value in measuring things. As he would repeat often to us, *"What gets measured gets improved."* I've heard others say, what gets measured gets managed, and therefore can get improved. That may be so, but when you are dealing with hyper-competitive elite athletes, simply measuring it is usually enough. Pro athletes are so driven that they just need to see the target and have it made very clear, then competitive instincts take over. What gets made visually clear, gets chased. If it doesn't, as a coach, you may need to ask yourself if you have the right guys in the room. As a player, you may need to ask yourself that same question. Don't you want to improve? The question is, what measurables are you chasing?

Setting the Mark

It was our last training camp practice before our first preseason game. I don't know if it was because I was young or if it was because Dan's level of practice intensity was so new to me, but that first training camp with Dan ended up being the most physically and mentally challenging camp of my entire career. By the end of those first two weeks of two-a-days, my body and maybe more so mind were spent. A preseason game was a welcome break. It would be the first time in two weeks we would actually get to block someone other than our own teammates. The first time that we would be out on the field for real, wearing our real uniforms, in front of a real crowd. No coaches jumping in to correct and adjust. It was time to see how we measured up against a real opponent. Time to see how we measured up against our own standards. In order to do that, we needed to know what those standards were.

No Breezy Preseason Games for Me

This was the first meeting of camp when we didn't review the tape of the previous practice. We finally had a game to prepare for, so there were a few housekeeping items that needed to be addressed. Up first was the play rotation. Because this was preseason, the emphasis was still on evaluating first, winning second. And because this was our first of two preseason games, starters playing time would take a back seat to those that needed a much greater opportunity to be evaluated. All starters except me. All other starters were scheduled to play only the first quarter. I was to play the first three. This decision was for three very real, very understandable reasons:

1. It was my first year and game as the team's real starting center. I didn't have years of seniority under my belt.

2. I was the center. Dan was new, and so was his whole system of blocking and calls. All the classroom work and practice reps were great, but nothing replaces real game experience. I didn't have any, so I needed as much as possible.

3. Because I was so new, I was still under heavy evaluation. I needed to prove I belonged in this group. I didn't have very much past film at all for this new coaching staff to go on, so I had to show them I was their guy.

I was good with all that. Some vets get to the point in their career that preseason games become an inconvenience, something they may even look to get out of playing. I never got to that place. Those three reasons kept changing and evolving throughout my years, but the three quarters of play remained consistent. My preseason games were always long and always real. I learned to not want it any other way. I love to play the game. Even preseason was a chance to play more and improve. Once we got the rotation out of the way and the contingency rotation in place, it was time to outline and discuss two things that would end up dictating our level of play for the remainder of my career: expectations and evaluations

You Need Objectivity in Measurables

As Dan talked, it became clear that one dictated the other. Our job was to do our job, and that's exactly what we would be graded on. Offensive line can be a tricky position to specifically measure. Nearly every other position in all of sports has very clear cut statistical categories that are universally accepted as measurable for performance evaluation. The only hard stats an offensive lineman racks up in the league's official documentation are penalties. Imagine that! The only measurables that the world ever sees in regard to your performance are negative. A good performance to the outside observer is the absence of ever hearing or knowing about what you did. That can make it very hard to have tangible appreciation for your work. Dan made sure, internally anyway, that wasn't the case.

The trick is making those measurables as objective as possible. It's also vital to:

1. Make them extremely clear to all, so that there is absolutely no confusion about what they are and how they will be viewed.

2. Make sure the WHY is clearly stated and accepted by all.

Without those two parameters, you end up with:

1. A hazy mark, leaving people unclear of where to aim.

2. Measurables that may not be bought into, or worse, are fought against.

Dan started by throwing an aggressive gauntlet down.

> **"We see a 90% grade or better as being a winning performance. That's what we expect from you here."**

90% for a passing grade seemed pretty high. What was unique, though, was his phrasing. There was no PASSING grade. There was a WINNING grade. Was your performance good enough to win with? That's all that mattered. In 2003, Dan set that mark at 90%. You had to do your job at a winning level 9 out of every 10 plays you completed. The mark was set high and made very clear.

"There are two things we are looking for in a winning play."

He then turned on an old school projector that lit up the white grease board outlining what a winning play consisted of. The image before us looked like this:

A WINNING PLAY

1. MENTAL

   a. ALIGNMENT

   b. ASSIGNMENT

Those two things were completely objective and entirely within our control. You either lined up right and went to the right person to block, or you didn't. It was pretty hard to question those parameters. There was really no judgment or interpretation needed. Dan merely recorded whether you did those two things or not. Simple. Clear.

2. PHYSICAL

PREVENTED YOUR PLAYER FROM DISRUPTING THE PLAY

That was it. Now, you could argue that this point was a little more subjective, but the wording was such that it kept things pretty clear. Did your inability to physically do your job negatively affect the play from doing what it was intended to do? When you look at that tightly defined statement, it gets much harder to not clearly see whether you physically did your job or not.

That was it. Clear and simple. The mark was set, and the parameters to hit the mark were laid out in clear, understandable language. This was one of the very few times Dan did not leave the door open for our input. He threw the gauntlet down. He didn't want us to manipulate the bar and reword it to fit our liking. I see now why sometimes it's so much more powerful to have a challenge imposed on you from an outside source.

Dan wasn't interested in what we thought a winning play was, but he made sure we CLEARLY understood what the club saw as a winning play as well as how our performance would be graded accordingly. He also made sure we all fully acknowledged that understanding and that we accepted it. Clarity and understanding were key, as was acceptance. Without those, measurables become an exercise in futility.

Doing your job gave you a plus (+) for that play. Failure to do so gave you a minus (-). You obviously wanted to see more pluses than minuses when you opened up your grade sheet from the previous game. To get the goodies we were about to be introduced to, you wanted pluses AT LEAST nine out of every ten plays.

Playing for Peanuts...Rolled in Caramel and a Few Other Ingredients

There's getting your paycheck, then there's earning your PayDay. One is contractually obliged; the other is earned only by your performance. One you can get your agent to deal with; the other, only you can achieve. One feeds your family; the other feeds your pride. It's funny how a $2 incentive can be so powerful, but that's just what the next topic of discussion by Dan proved.

He had a bag with him. It was a small bag and looked similar to one of those hotel cloth bags you might put your shoes in to get them polished. I'm almost certain that's not where that bag was from, but it was the only comparable I could think of at the time. You could tell by both the searching of his hand and the rustling sound that there were a few small items in there. He was searching by feel alone. He obviously knew exactly what he was looking for. He pulled his hand out to reveal a fully wrapped PayDay candy bar. Now, I hadn't known Dan very long yet, but I already knew the man enough to know he was not the type to pack candy bars in his bag for impulsive mid-day snacking. Dan didn't do anything impulsive, and eating candy bars just didn't fit his M.O. So... what was going on here?

He held the bar up near his face, exposing the PayDay logo to us in such meticulous fashion that it looked like he was setting up to do an infomercial.

"Hi, my name is Dan Dorazio, and I love PayDay bars." He didn't say any of that, and he definitely didn't unwrap it and dive in. He wanted to explain rewards — rewards for a job well done.

A PayDay bar would be awarded to any player that put out a winning performance the previous game. You truly earned your PayDay. It's amazing what happens in a room of competitive people when some get to eat their PayDay bar while others sit empty handed. It may be a $2 stick of salted peanuts rolled in caramel, surrounding a firm nougat-like center, but it's what it represented that made all the difference. It was a tangible, public acknowledgment of a job well done. I personally dislike PayDay bars, but for some reason, they always tasted amazing during those meetings. It was that satisfying taste of a job well done.

The Winning Performance Equation

"Play at a level that your opponent is unwilling or unable to match."

There were other parameters required to earn a winning performance as well. Your sack ratio and pressure ratio needed to be in order. Again, clear targets with straight forward objective parameters.

An acceptable sack ratio throughout the course of a season was 1/125. Meaning, if you gave up a sack in less than one out of one hundred and twenty-five throwing play snaps, you were playing winning football. That again was broken down to a very clear, very objective definition. Each and every passing play had a planned time frame that it was expected to take. For example, 662 x pony trade (it's a bunch of nonsense, I know) was a 2.8 ball. All that means is that the play is designed to have the quarterback throw the ball in 2.8 seconds. That .8 sounds like splitting hairs, but in the world of pass protection, every tenth of a second matters, and you learn to 'feel' the difference between tenths very quickly. So, on that particular play, a sack would have to be given up in that time frame for it to have counted. If the quarterback held onto the ball for four seconds – that sack was on him. Clear, simple, objective. The stop watch tells you if you did well or not. Dan just recorded it.

Quarterback hurries, pressures, and hits presented the same scenario as sacks, only the ratio was a little more forgiving. The ratio of 1/25 passing plays was acceptable. Again, what equaled a pressure, hit, or hurry was predicated on the time allotted for that play. Did you prevent your man from doing any of these things to our quarterback in the designed play time frame? If so, from a grade perspective, all good. Please don't misunderstand, getting a (+) didn't always mean there weren't things to be improved on that play, but it did mean you fit the outlined, objective-based parameter of grading.

To fully qualify for your prized PayDay bar required fulfilling the following:

1. 90% or higher grade

2. Pressure ratio of 1/25 or better

3. Sack ratio of 1/125 or better – You really couldn't give up a sack and earn a PayDay bar. That would require us throwing the ball more

than 125 times in a game! The most plays I had ever run in one game in my entire career was 77. Bottom line: to get a PayDay – NO SACKS.

4.   Finally, NO mental errors. This was again very objective. If you went the wrong way, went to the wrong person, or got a mentally driven penalty (offsides, illegal procedure, etc.) a PayDay was off the table.

There it was. All laid out very clearly. The standard that was expected and exactly what it took to meet it. You can't ask for more than that. It didn't require Dan's interpretation of how I played. All he had to do was record how our play measured up. I pretty much knew my grade the second the last play of the night was run. I knew whether I went the right way or not. I knew how many times my assignment disrupted the play. I clearly knew if I had mental penalties. The only uncertainty sometimes was in the sacks, hurries, hits, and pressure. You do get an amazing feel for fractions of seconds, but even still, sometimes you're not totally sure. You also have no idea what else was going on behind you during the play. What the quarterback or other players may have done to alter where that play went and ended up. Either way, you knew while watching film the next day that the evaluation had already been made based on what you did. The parameters were already set. I wasn't waiting for Dan to come up with my grade. He would merely be compiling what I did.

> **I made my grade. We all do.**

Set the Bar High, Then Raise It Higher

"Good, better, best, never let it rest,

'til your good is better, and your better is best."

> *~ Dan at the first meeting of every training camp*

During the very first workout of my second off-season with Dan, he said, *"Angus, let me tell you something. Last year, you learned how to work out. This year, we can start training."*

It was said tongue in cheek, I think, but Dan always cloaked his humor so well that you never could be 100% sure. He liked it that way and looking back, I did, too. It made simple statements like that one memorable more than 15 years later. You were sure he was joking, just never 100% sure. A true art. Either way, that statement was true on many levels. He did crank the workouts up. Yes, the box was still there, and yes, we still did our various sets equaling forty jumps per workout — but everything got harder. He turned the intensity up. He added more drills and allowed less rest. He demanded more effort and forgave less error. He became relentless with both his demands and his scrutiny. Even though I never thought I could give any more or could do any better, somehow, I always did.

> **You rise to the demands and expectations that are placed on you. Once you reach a certain bar, the only way to continue growth is to raise that bar more. If you are always hitting your mark, the mark is too low. Time to bump it up.**

During that first off-season, those workouts nearly killed me. I adapted to the stress and demands, and soon they became normal. Improvement doesn't happen when things become and remain normal, though. Complacency sets in, and you very quickly stop pushing, stop improving, stop growing. Then, the whole process becomes a sequence of useless routines — a waste of time. Dan always understood that and made sure he kept an objective view on when we needed that bar raised. That goes for everything that really matters in your life, too. It needs to be objectively measured; a bar needs to be set, and once achieved, that bar needs to be bumped up, or comfort will take over, and real growth will quickly cease.

> **"We need five guys that are going to have a relentless desire to improve every day. And that's what toughness is."**
>
> **~ Dan**

In 2003, we were "learning how to work out." By 2006, getting a 90% grade had become the norm, to the point I think Dan may have received a wholesaler's discount with Hersey's due to the heavy volume of PayDay bars he was having to buy.

The only logical move was to bump it up. Not just to save Dan a few bucks on purchases, but to force us to chase a new target — a harder target.

The New Standard

To play winning football, you now had to do your job by all the parameters outlined before but upped to 9.2 plays out of every 10. Ninety-two percent! That's not just playing pretty solid football; that's winning. We would play maybe 60 plays in a game. That's 56 times out of every 60 that you performed at a level that was good enough to win with. Imagine doing 56 out of every 60 acts of your day at that level. That means you are winning in life. That's kicking some serious ass. Competitive people will naturally chase the bar that is set. Make that bar high and watch them do what it takes to get there, then bump it up and watch them somehow give more. It's incredible to see, but that's just what happened.

Our grades slowly moved as a group from the low 90s before 2006 to the mid-90s after. Nothing else had changed, just the bar, and our competitive response to it. Never underestimate the power of setting a seemingly impossible standard. Make it real, make it clear, make it objective, and make it public. You'd be shocked at what that challenge can do to facilitate changes necessary to meet that previously unrealistic goal — then raise it again. Competitive people want to be challenged. Just make sure you've learned how to work-out before you really start training. It's great to have the drive, but you also need to have the gas built up to get it done.

Ruthlessly Adhere to the Standards Set

Every single end to a season that doesn't finish with a championship is almost always the exact same — full of disappointment for what didn't get done and uncertainty about the inevitable changes that will definitely get made. There are a litany of exit interviews, each seeming to convey a feeling of hope that we would both be back next year to give it another go. It was always a depressing feeling, going through the mandatory motions of signing your playbook back in to your coach, filling out your off-season address info for the player personnel guy, and signing all your issued equipment and gear back to 'Kato,' our great equipment guy. That sign-in was always the last. 'Kato' was the gatekeeper. He held the all-powerful stack of final game cheques. In order to receive yours, your sheet had to be signed by everyone, proving you'd returned everything and had done everything required. Only after showing proof of task AND returning all team-issued gear would you be granted your final pay, then you were free to leave. Very methodic. Very clinical, and when you didn't win, it's very somber. It sucked.

What I learned after that 2006 Championship was that winning changes everything. All those procedures still had to be done of course, but the emotions, mood, and overall experience were completely different. The whole day was full of congratulations and smiles. The final team meeting was less a debriefing and much more of a party planning event. What mattered now was not being honest about the uncertainty of each and every one of our futures but making sure we all knew where we needed to be and when we needed to be there for the organized celebrations and events. Most of the structured necessities that seemed so important in previous years somehow just didn't seem to matter as much. Most people kept their issued gear from the year as mementos, and for some reason (because we'd won), now that was fine. Again, winning changes things.

Our final positional meeting was simply a smile and hug fest. It may have been the only time I can ever remember in my entire career that Dan didn't have our grades ready and posted. We never even watched the film. How we played didn't seem that important right now. We won. That's all that mattered — then I opened the envelope.

Unexpected Mail

It showed up maybe 10 days following our Grey Cup win. It was an 8"x10" official BC Lions branded envelope. My name and address were hand written in Dan's all too familiar, less than perfect penmanship. I wasn't quite sure what to expect. We had already had our downtown Grey Cup celebration party. All the photos and congratulations had been taken and shared. Most out of town players had already left for home. Our facility, which only a week ago was the most action- packed, energy-filled building in the city, was now all but a ghost town. It was a magical ride for sure, but the come down had already begun. The season was now over. It was all wrapped up. This was early December and our off-season work wouldn't even begin until late February. Unless this was the world's largest Christmas card, I honestly didn't know what Dan was mailing me. Again, I should have guessed.

It wasn't a Christmas card — it was my grade sheet. No congratulations or praise. No subjective discussion on what we had just accomplished. That was all done in person. This was what I actually did in the game. This was my work. The honest, objective review and evaluation of my work. Nothing more, and definitely nothing less.

I knew I had played a fair game. "Fair" is a Dan word that I have never really come to truly understand. He would say a play or performance was "fair," "very fair," "somewhat fair," "almost fair," and a whole litany of other versions of the word. It got to the point that I lost all understanding of what was good or not. My life with Dan seemed to constantly live somewhere in the "fair" spectrum. So, with that said, I confidently felt my performance in that championship game was "fair." Take that for whatever you want to take it for. That's what I ended up doing with the word.

I gave up no sacks or hits. I MAY have given up a pressure. Other than that, I knew I played pretty well. I was actually excited to see how the tape matched my memory.

I was right: one pressure. It was a scramble. I remember the play well. We ended up gaining good yardage on it, but I created a scramble nonetheless. Everything else looked pretty in line with my recollection, then I saw it — a penalty. I didn't get a penalty!

The Truth Hurts

I flipped through the pages to find the play in question. 662 x – rain poison. REID – HOLDING. What? I didn't get a holding call. Now you need to know, Dan handwrote each and every play from the game. Every single piece of information we ever received from Dan was handwritten. This was not some official CFL game day fact sheet. This whole thing was Dan's creation. HOLDING. No way! There was a little space for comments beside the play. In tiny print, Dan had written, *"This is holding."* I had NOT gotten a holding penalty that game. Dan had given me a holding penalty. In that moment, I couldn't remember the play. I just remember being furious! We just won the Grey Cup, and he's making up holding penalties? Seriously? What made it worse was that my grade came in at 91%. One percent short of a winning performance. That one minus difference came from a holding penalty that Dan invented. We won the Grey Cup! Who cares about a penalty that never got called and that never affected the play?

I called my buddy Bobby Singh. *"Bobby, did you get your grade sheet in the mail?"*

"Ha ha ha. Yup! Crazy, right?" Bobby pretty much laughs at everything. He's one of the best personalities you will ever be around. A truly larger than life personality that always seems to be having fun. *"I can't believe he actually mailed us our PayDay bars! He's crazy!"*

Wait. What? Dan mailed out PayDay bars? Three things popped into my head:

1. Dan really is nuts, just like the bars themselves. What a guy. He stays true to what he says and always delivers on his word.

2. Bobby got a bar, and I didn't. I was embarrassed, jealous, and pissed.

3. Why would Dan fail to give me a PayDay bar due to a penalty he created? Just mail everyone a bar! We won the Cup!

I lied to Bob and agreed that it was ridiculous that Dan fulfilled his word on rewards to this extent. Getting a PayDay in the mail was a hilarious story that I didn't want to be left out of. Besides, nobody would ever know. Our next group meeting would be at training camp next year. Any factual evidence would be neatly archived and probably never brought up again.

Unfinished Business

The next morning, I drove out to the facility. I needed to watch the game. More to the point, I needed to see this coach inflicted holding penalty. The facility was empty. The coaches were gone, but the film was easy to find. It was still all loaded up in our meeting room, probably from Dan's last review. I went in telling myself to sit back and watch the game, to enjoy reliving the whole experience — the highs, the lows, and ultimately the victory that we had fought so hard for. Intentions are one thing; single minded focus is another. I couldn't stop myself. All I wanted to do was see this play. To see why Dan would screw me out of a PayDay. Why would he not just give me the grade? We won the Grey Cup!

Found It

It was the sixth play of the second quarter, second down and 7 yards to go. 662 x- rain poison. It's a straight drop back passing play. Simple, basic, pocket pass protection (although Dan would kill me for calling what we made for the quarterback a pocket). He demanded using the word "DISH." Offensive line coaches would get the significance of that subtle difference in phrasing. Either way, it was a passing play. Big Adriano Belli, the man the Lions traded away to acquire me so many years earlier was lined up right over me. He charged hard at me and caught me off guard and not in the best position to respond. Before I knew it, I was on my heels with my upper body quickly getting steamrolled backwards. I was getting runover. It happened too fast for me to pop my feet back and recover. I was going down and down fast. If pancakes are universally seen as lineman domination, a reverse pancake is absolute lineman humiliation. I was just about there. I did what I had to do to save the play. I felt my body falling backwards, so I grabbed onto Adriano as tightly as I could and made sure he came down with me. Instead of just running directly over me en route to the quarterback, I made sure he completed the sacred art of pancaking by forcing him to body splash on top of me. Embarrassing? Yes. Play saving? Absolutely. You do what you have to do sometimes. There were no flags; there was no pressure on the quarterback, so in my mind, there was no minus, and definitely no penalty. Did my technique need correcting? One hundred percent. Was it a good play? No way, but it fit the parameters of a plus — then I watched it again.

On closer review it became painfully clear that I pulled Adriano down with my hands way outside his shoulders. My hands were wide. It was a blatant hold that was simply missed by the officials. I watched it a third time, and the reality just kept getting worse. It wasn't just a hold; it was a bad hold. Dan didn't give me a holding penalty. I did. He just marked down what happened. Always honest. Always objective. Always consistent...even when reviewing a championship win. I may have thought he should have given me a PayDay bar, but the honest truth was that I hadn't earned one. The standard was the standard. I hadn't measured up. He wasn't being mean. He was just being objectively honest.

The Takeaway

Dan taught me to set standards high and to ruthlessly adhere to them — to never adjust the standard because of a situation. It's your job to meet the standard, not the standard's job to meet you.

THE POWER OF PUBLIC ACCOUNTABILITY

"Every time you put your hand on the ground, you are signing your signature."

~ Dan

I was always at work early. I've just always been a morning person. First meeting of the day would start at 9 a.m., so I would routinely be there by 7 a.m., sometimes to get a morning workout in, sometimes to get treatment, sometimes to watch some extra film, and sometimes just because I like being at places early. I hate ever feeling rushed.

What I did each morning varied throughout my career based on what was most important and needed to get done on any given day. I didn't have a standard morning routine, nothing I could admittedly state I did consistently throughout my career. Nothing, except one. The first day back after a game, my very first order of business was to check the grades. My personal grade sheet would be waiting for me in my locker stall. I'd give it a quick look to make sure it matched up to my memory of my performance. It almost always did. Remember, Dan didn't give us our grades; our own performance did.

There for All to See

Once I confirmed the grade I already pretty much knew, it was on to what really mattered. How did everyone else do? Our meeting room may have been full of positive statements reminding us what it means to be an offensive lineman, but the morning after a game, there was only one posted board that mattered – our publicly displayed grades.

It was for all to see that wanted to poke their heads in and take a peek. It listed every lineman that played in the game and broke down all the criteria that got measured. What mattered most was the percentage. Did you play a winning game? Did you grade higher than 92%, give up zero sacks, and play penalty free? We're all told to compete only with ourselves, that's solid advice, but it's impossible to follow . Competitive people need an external challenge and comparable measuring stick. Dan would always remind us that, *"Every time you put your hand on the ground you [were] signing your signature."* Players should be proud of their work. You should want your teammates and anyone else that takes a peek to see what you have done and how it measures up, especially when the measurables are so objective and consistent. It may not be the right way to gauge yourself, but I can tell you it works. You care how you stack up against your peers. You care that they will all see how they stack up against you. You care that everyone else on the team will know, too. Public accountability for your performance to all of your teammates is a powerful thing. It drives you to perform better and brings out the very best in your ability. When you know your work of art is hanging for all to see, you make sure they see the very best that you've got.

Sweetening the Deal

Dan may never have actually talked about "pancake" blocks, but make no mistake about it, physical domination of your man was not only acknowledged, but deliciously rewarded. Back in his little hotel shoe shine looking bag his hand dove. There was obviously still more than one item down there, but he quickly located his next discussion point. Out came a Nestlé Crunch bar. Like filming another infomercial, Dan held the bar high for us all to see, *"This Crunch bar will be awarded each game to the player that records the most green dots."* Green dots? What the heck are green dots?

> **Green dots were any form of domination where your block went above and beyond the basic standard expectation.**

Breaking Down Domination.
Maximizing Opportunities to Shine.

"THAT'S kicking some ass!!"

~ Dan

As with absolutely everything else he did, Dan had a detailed description of exactly what was meant by what he was presenting. Again, in classic Dan form, there were five separate categories that classified as opportunities to earn a green dot.

1. DOWNFIELD BLOCKS
2. DECLEATERS
3. DOMINATION BLOCKS
4. CUT BLOCKS
5. KNOCKDOWNS

They sound simple enough, but Dan defined each and every one for us.

DOWNFIELD BLOCKS – Any block that is secondary to your initial assignment. It is made down the field somewhere on the second level of the defensive. It's an extra effort block that can sometimes make the difference on a big play.

DECLEATERS – This would be the initial phase of a traditional "pancake" block — any block where you physically lifted the defender off the ground to the point that BOTH his cleats came off the ground. This block usually resulted in the defender ending up flat on his back. A decleater is one of the most visibly impressive things to see on a football game film.

DOMINATION BLOCKS – If a decleater is one of the most impressive things to watch, a domination block is probably the most respected. This is any block where you literally take the defender for a ride. You run him wherever you want. In classic meticulous Dan form, to technically qualify for a domination block, you had to drive your defender AT LEAST 5 yards after initial contact. Again, he kept things very specific and objectively measurable. No arguments. Just reality.

CUT BLOCKS – Any block where you legally cut the defender's legs to the point that they ended up on the ground. There would be lots of heated debates over the years from players demanding green dots from Dan for their cut blocks that weren't awarded. If the player did not end up on the ground, no green dot was issued. It may very well have been a great block and may have been what sprung the play, but objectively rewarding what was tightly defined was big. It kept everything consistent and fair for all.

KNOCKDOWNS – These were ANY blocks that resulted in the defender ending up on the ground. Dan was huge on rewarding anything that got a defender to have to expend precious energy having to pick himself up off the turf. Continually having to pick yourself up again and again becomes both physically and, sometimes more importantly, psychologically draining.

There you had it. No pancakes, but five separate ways to go above and beyond your basic job description. Five separate ways to earn green dots. Five separate ways to compete for the weekly award of delicious milk chocolate filled with crisped rice. Having so many different opportunities to gather green dots was a brilliant play on Dan's part. It really did allow anybody the chance to be the week's Crunch winner. We had some monsters that simply dominated nearly every player they ever put their hands on. We also had many plays that were drawn up for our back side to always cut block their inside defenders. Certain players and certain plays lent themselves naturally to more opportunities for one celebrated block or the other. No matter how hard I tried, I simply couldn't maul many guys to the domination block standards. Also, playing center meant I was always front side on every single wide zone running play, giving me a zero percent chance of ever having a cut block option no matter which way we ran it. Some blocks lent themselves better to certain players and certain plays. The ability to get green dots from so many different options, though, allowed each of us endless opportunities to compete for the weekly bar. You can always work to knock down your defender or hustle to the second level to make that next block. Some green dots were more film envious than others, but they all mattered and were all recorded.

Keeping Consistent – The Power of Color

After the Crunch bar and green dot parameters were explained, the bag with the bar thrown back in it was placed neatly on the ground. Dan had another explanation to walk us through. This time the visual came from a single piece of paper. At least I thought it was a single piece of paper. Dan dug through his leather covered file folder and removed an 8"x10" white sheet. He then began to unfold it and unfold it and unfold it. What I initially thought was a single sheet turned out to be four sheets scotch taped together. Dan now held between his two outstretched arms a long four-page landscaped connected chart. At first glance, all I could see were multiple horizontal lines of varying lengths in groups of three, with each chunk having one green, one red, and one brown colored row.

As he always did, Dan went on to explain.

"Men, this is a colored record of your season. The green dots represent any play that we just went over. All the good stuff. The red dots represent any pressure, hurry, hit, or sack that you've surrendered, the not so good stuff. The brown row right here, that represents any mental error or penalty you have committed. Keeping in line with the color – that's the real shitty stuff."

As he spoke, I focused closer on the chart. It was an actual document from his previous season in Calgary. I could now see all the names — Jamie Crysdale, Jay McNeil, Fred Childress, etc. Wow! I remember thinking, this man not only tracks absolutely everything, but he also keeps absolutely everything! That sheet would end up hanging on our wall just below our grades. The visual impact of seeing how your colors measured up against your fellow mates may have been even more impactful than the percentage numbers that hung above. As the season went on, our columns grew. The only question was, which colored horse was leading the charge and by how much?

More than Just Visual Competition

It became a very competitive race, watching those green lines expand horizontally outwards. Yes, the weekly Crunch bar was awarded, but the real bragging rights came with the year-end completion of your colored masterpiece. Who would reign as the Green Dot King? Who would win the shortest red line? The shortest brown line? Each carried its own visual bragging rights and came with a sense of pride. Just like the chocolate bars, it's fascinating what a five-cent piece of paper with some Sharpie colored columns can do for competitiveness and pride. That sheet was a huge deal in our world. It was our ongoing work hung for all to see in simple color-coded fashion. A visual representation of what we achieved that season – for better or worse.

Acknowledging Perfection: The Eraser

Every target has to have a bullseye. The point of perfection. I don't believe you can show a competitive person a target without it. Standards are important, but ultimately, perfection is what we are all chasing. Even if perfection is technically not possible, a level seen as such needs to be presented. The ultimate carrot needs to be known. That's exactly what Dan went fishing for back in that smallish cloth bag.. This was to be the last item addressed regarding expectations and evaluations. Dan's hand found what it was searching for. Unlike the PayDay and Crunch bar though, he didn't bring the item out right away. He kept his right hand buried in that sack, holding firmly to the pièce de résistance — the award that was regarded above all else. In short, it was the mark of offensive lineman perfection.

"Men," he scanned the room as he held a long pause, *"every once in a while, we will see a performance out there that is special. Not just great, but truly special."* He paused again, scanned the room once more, and locked eyes with each and every one of us.

He was a master at holding pauses and grabbing our attention. *"Special performances demand special acknowledgments. Now, I've got to tell you, we don't hand these out very often. In order to win this, you've got to play some perfect football. You see this right here?"* He then pulled his hand out of the sack. I assumed it was going to be another edible sugar laced product. Not this time. Dan held up a cheap looking, run of the mill white board eraser. I had no idea in that moment how prized that $2 Office Depot product would become over the remainder of my career.

"This right here, men, is the ERASER award." He motioned his outstretched arm from left to right like a lawyer showing evidence to a jury in a courtroom. ***"In order to qualify for this, you need to grade out at 100%. This symbolizes the fact that you not only played mistake-free football, but you also completely erased your opponent from the game."*** In all my years of playing, I had never heard domination explained like that

before. You made it so he didn't even exist out there. What a powerful metaphor for dominance! The eraser became our mark of perfection.

He was bang on, too. Those erasers didn't get handed out often. Maybe a few times a year. In the 11 seasons I played with Dan, I won four erasers. The last two being the most special. My second to the last one was earned our final game of the 2010 regular season —the year I battled my way back on the field after my supposed career ending foot injury. Playing a perfect game on my final outing was the very best statement I could make heading into that year-end conversation.

The last eraser was earned on the final game I ever played. I didn't know it at the time, but the 2012 Western Final ended up being it for me. My career ending back injury sidelined me for the entire following season. Those last two erasers sit proudly in my office to this very day. They may have just been cheap office necessities with my name, game date, and the word "ERASER" handwritten and scotch taped to the front, but to me, they are a cherished reminder that on those days, on the field, I was perfect.

Every standard has to have a bullseye. A level of perfection that one can chase. As much as true perfection can never truly be reached, Dan believed in acknowledging work that represented effort that was as close to it as humanly possible. As with Dan's other awards, it wasn't the grandness or monetary value of them that made them prized; it was what they represented that mattered. **A reward for a job well done is much less about the award itself and more about the acknowledgment that you have accomplished something special. Football, just like life, is hard. It's important to take the time to appreciate extraordinary moments. As busy as Dan always kept himself, he always paused to make sure he did that when our play warranted it. I've never forgotten that.**

Never Say Never

As far as grading was concerned, I had never seen Dan bend, compromise, or allow a sound argument to persuade him to change an objectively based grade. It just didn't happen — until that one time when it did.

It was late 2007. We had just beaten the Calgary Stampeders at home to go 9–3–1. We would end up going 14–3–1 that season, one game short of the Grey Cup that year, losing a heartbreaking Western Final to the Saskatchewan RoughRiders. We may not have won a championship that year, but I would confidently state that in terms of talent, that was the very best BC Lions team I ever played on. That team was chock-full of All-Stars. Not just talented athletes, but guys that really knew how to play the game. Guys like Rob Murphy.

"Murph" came to us the previous season following a 7-year run in the NFL. He was a big brute of an offensive tackle that played the game the way you would have expected him to by looking at his pedigree. "Murph" was from Cincinnati. Football was in his blood. His old man was a running back at the University of Miami. Rob went and played at famed Moeller High before taking his talents to Columbus. He was a two-time All-American at The Ohio State University and was, by all accounts, a true "football player." By the time he came to us, there wasn't much he hadn't seen or done on the field. He really knew the game at a level one can only understand if it's what they have grown up doing their entire life. His instincts for what to do, when to do it, and when to adjust were incredible. A lifetime of coaching could never get me to the place where a lifetime of playing had gotten Rob. From a coaching perspective, he was Dan's favorite the second he showed up. It only made sense. Dan now had a player that had all the football knowledge and instincts already ingrained. He was a finished product right out of the box. On top of all of that – Rob delivered.

Murph took our league by storm. In his rookie season, he was voted unanimously the Top Lineman in our entire league. With reporters doing the voting, and a position that falls short on common stats, winning that award in your first year is completely unheard of. That's the kind of dominant impact Rob made. He played football the old way. He beat people up out there. He was so good that he did something I never thought previously possible, and he never even had to put his pads on to get it done.

I was in at my usual 7–7:15 that Monday morning. A quick glance at my grade sheet waiting patiently for me on the chair inside my locker stall brought an anticipated smile to my face. 94%. No sacks. No pressures. No mental errors. Solid. Better than solid actually. I played a fantastic game, just as I had remembered it. It's a great feeling when the tape matches your recollection. The longer I played, the more accurate I got at pegging my grade long before having to look at it. Up next, seeing how my mates faired. This ritual was always easier after the assurance that your performance was PayDay worthy. We had won and had beaten a good Calgary team. I knew we played well as a group and was expecting solid grades across the board. I was right…with one dramatic exception. Rob Murphy. Rob graded 87%. A fair grade for most, but when you're the most dominant lineman in the league, and everyone else graded 90+, that 87% sticks out like a sore thumb. I was shocked. It may very well have been the lowest grade Rob ever received — but it didn't last long.

I went about the rest of my morning. A quick hot tub soak to loosen up some sore day after muscles, then I hit the gym for a quick workout. I didn't give those grades another thought. It wasn't until I got back to my locker stall post-shower that I heard all the whispering. Just because we're huge 300 lb. men does not mean we are beyond natural school yard gossip.

"Have you seen the grade board?" That was the question multiple people were directing my way.

"Yeah, why?"

"You see Murph's grade?" It was like nobody could believe it was possible for Rob Murphy to ever miss the mark. I knew it was unusual, but I was surprised at what a big deal it was.

"Yeah," I responded. *"I was surprised, too. 87%. Wow! He must have really had an off day."*

"No…you need to come see this." It was said as if someone had just found a unicorn or some other previously imagined impossibility.

Back to our meeting room I went. Like school girls excited to see my response, a few of my mates followed. It was a unicorn! At least in respect to a previously believed impossibility. Rob's grade was now 93%! In standard old school Dan form, the 87 had been covered up with White-Out, and a new 93% had been written over top. It was unprecedented! I had never seen a grade changed before and honestly, I don't believe I've ever seen it done since.

At some point early that morning Rob had come in to privately review his game with Dan, a practice many of us had done from time to time, especially if there was something you struggled with that would require a little more personal discussion than our group meetings would allow time for. Rob obviously disagreed with Dan's review of his performance, again, as many of us did from time to time. The only difference was that this time Dan changed his mind and agreed with Rob. THAT had never happened!

At first, I thought he was just playing favorites. That because Rob was the league's top lineman Dan cut him some slack and made the adjustment to make sure Rob was acknowledged accordingly…then we watched the film. There were three plays that were changed. At first it was easy to see why Dan would have graded each as a minus, then we broke them down and discussed them. Rob broke all the rules on those three plays. He did everything wrong from a standard coaching perspective, but what he did do on each actually helped the play beyond his established role. Rob was so smart that he improvised and adjusted. He did things out there that were technically wrong but ended up being the only way of making sure the play worked. What looked like a mistake by anyone else, became new coaching points for the rest of us. Even Dan didn't see them as such until Rob went up and explained his actions and the reasons behind them. That is when a statement Dan would start every training camp telling us finally made sense to me.

"Men, I need you to know I will treat each and every one of you fairly as individuals…but as players…I cannot treat you all the same."

Murph played football at a much different level than I did, and Dan coached him appropriately. He did that with all of us. I came to learn how important that phrase from Dan really was. We are not all the same. For Dan to have coached us all the same would have been unfair to each of us.

Dan taught me to make sure to treat everyone fairly, no matter what, but that it's unfair to treat everyone the same. And as my play changed, so did Dan's coaching.

Even the "Tried and True" Can Fail

"Dan, we're getting killed off the front side!" I was furious. Not so much at anything I was doing wrong, but more at the fact that we were getting exploited, and there was nothing we could do about it.

"You just worry about keeping your eyes where they belong. Let me worry about the front side," Dan barked back in an unusually hot-tempered game day tone. As frustrated as I was, I think Dan was more so.

It was July 29, 2006. We were on the road playing in Toronto, and the Argos had finally exploited a major weakness in our pass protection system. Since Dan's arrival in 2003, our basic drop back pass blocking system had been completely overhauled. Most teams still had their lineman block the man in front of them and allowed their free lineman (usually the center) to pop back, pick up any blitzing linebacker, or help out a fellow lineman in need. Dan brought to us a true zone pass blocking system that has since become common place, but in 2003, it was a huge shift in pass blocking philosophy. With zone blocking, we cut our line in half. Front side was the guard and tackle that was aligned to the side the quarterback would be facing to throw. Back side was always myself and the guard and tackle to the quarterback's back – his blind side.

Our front side guard and tackle would simply be BIG ON BIG, meaning they just needed to block the defensive lineman in front of them. Pretty simple. They would usually also have a running back to help pick up any extra man that might blitz.

The back side zone philosophy was also very simple in concept...it was adhering to all of its disciplines during the high pressure of a game that made it tricky. We were basically blocking space with our bodies and players with our eyes.

If the play was 662, that meant the quarterback's back side was going to be to the left. The right guard and right tackle would be, as Dan would call them, "independent contractors." They were on their own, mano a mano with their defender. The left guard, left tackle, and I would work as a team. Zone, or back side slide protection as it became known, required each of us to move as little as possible. We would ideally just kick one foot out of our stance (left foot if zone blocking left) to open ourselves just enough to physically cover the gap to our left, then we'd hunker down and not move! That sounds so easy, but trust me, the hardest thing in the world on a line of scrimmage is to sit in place. It takes tremendous discipline to avoid subconsciously drifting. Slide protection demands that each player stays in place or else huge holes get created for defenders to charge through. Just stay put, but keep your eyes glued to the gap to your left. Again, easier said than done. If done right, you'll have created a nice solid wall that has each gap accounted for. Now, it has a lot more complexities than that, but that's the general idea. The premise is simple: don't drift and never take your eyes off your wingman. You see, if a player makes an inside move on our left guard, that becomes my block. He keeps his eyes left in order to protect the gap to his left. We all trust that the man beside us has his eyes where they belong. This style of blocking requires a ton of trust and even more repetitions together to get comfortable with that trust.

We struggled for the first two years, our bodies and eyes subconsciously drifting at critical moments. Dan became ruthless with the never-ending repetitions on this protection. He scolded us for lazy eye placement and body drifting. Drill after drill after drill eventually ingrained the physical discipline we needed to be exactly where we were supposed to be every single time. As with all skill development, with proper practice over time we improved. Soon it began to resemble the film Dan had first showed us three years earlier during our vision building phase. We began, as Dan would often sarcastically say, to actually look like we knew what we were doing out there.

We were becoming so well trained that our back side slide looked like a well-oiled machine. Our three bodies hunkered right where you'd want them, and our eyes were firmly fixed on our wingman's inside. We had that back side locked down.

But in every strength, there lies its own inherent weakness. Toronto had just exploited ours. Instead of playing balanced, sound defense, they simply started using our system against us. On obvious passing downs when they wanted to bring pressure, they just overloaded the side away from our slide. Sometimes you could see it coming pre-snap, but other times it was too late to change anything. They would bring five hard charging defenders to the side away from our slide. We only had two linemen and possibly a running back to that side to protect. Pretty rough numbers to work with when trying to prevent your quarterback from getting his head knocked off. Meanwhile, they would occasionally rush a single player to the back side to keep containment. What we ended up with was a highly disciplined, great looking textbook three-man slide protection blocking one person, while two defenders came scot-free from the other side. That's the trouble sometimes with rules that don't allow adaptation — they get played against you. We had to do something.

The Key to Success: Adaptation

"Dan, how about this. Once I ensure we have no more than two defenders to the back side, what if I turn and help the front side? I can get that extra defender! We can solve this!"

"The guard has your eyes, Angus! You'll screw him if you take off!"

"I'll scream GONE! And I'll scream it loud enough that even YOU will hear it. The guard and tackle will know to tighten back and that inside help will be gone."

Dan paused for a moment. This was mid-way through our fourth season together, and I had never gotten this far with him on a proposed adjustment. He looked back at me then glanced over to the rest of the line. *"You guys okay with that?"*

"Yeah!" was their collective response.

"Okay, if you think you can do it. You just make damn sure that guard knows you're gone!" (Volume not only reflects confidence, but, on the field, sometimes simply ensures communications get heard.)

"No problem, coach."

That was that. Our system changed right then and there. We went back out, and sure enough Toronto went right back to it, but this time we shut it down. Then we shut it down again and then again. They finally stopped that nonsense because we were exploiting their system and getting the ball to our superstars. We crushed Toronto that day, and two things changed forever.

We adapted our slide protection system, freeing us from our own handcuffs and giving us more options. But more importantly for me, my "same" changed. For the first time in my career, Dan allowed me to not only give input on our system but actually allowed me to change it. I wasn't the same wide-eyed, confused center from three years ago; I had knowledge and experience now. I had grown, and the way Dan coached me had grown as well.

The Takeaway

That day and its sequence of events marked the beginning of many more discussions on system adaptations and technique tweaks that Dan and I would discuss throughout my career. It seemed that the longer I played the more open he became to my input and ideas. Dan treated us all fairly, but he couldn't treat us all the same. And our same was always changing, and as it changed, so did Dan's coaching. I was a different player each and every one of my 11 seasons with him, and looking back now, he coached me differently in every one of those years — always fairly, just not ever the same. The way it should be.

CALMNESS IS CONTAGIOUS

"Whoa, just slow down a second."

~ **Dan**

I couldn't stop my heel from pounding. Up and down, up and down it went. The more I tried to stop it, the faster it would go, like a sewing machine hammering out stitch after stitch. It was five minutes to kickoff. Well, five minutes until we had to start heading out for intros, etc. It was basically five minutes until this all got very real.

Week One Was Finally Here!

The season I had been prepping for, not just in the last four months with Dan, but really since the day I first donned pads, I would run out of the tunnel in a few minutes as the starting center for my childhood hometown team, the BC Lions. Yes, I had started two games the previous season, but now I WAS the starter. There's a big difference. At least in my mind there was. My time had finally arrived.

I sat at my locker trying to look as cool as all the seasoned vets around me. My nervous heel was my dead tell, though. I hadn't felt this in nearly three years — that intense nervous energy that builds just before action needs to be taken. Those few minutes are strange. All the work that can be done has already been done, anything more now would be counter-productive. But acting on and utilizing all that preparation would have to wait for the game to actually begin. You spend all week strategically building to this point. To the point where you have built up as much knowledge of not just the team you're facing, but the man you will be physically going to war against for the next three or so hours. In these few minutes, though, all you can do is wait. For the untrained mind, this quiet time can be deafening.

Football is a unique team sport in that you only ever play one game a week. The physical demands simply don't allow for multiple games over multiple days. Unlike basketball, baseball, or even hockey, a football game has a weekly build up — a schedule designed to layer one prep day upon another to methodically bring you to a boiling point on game day. A place where physically and mentally you are completely ready to battle, not just the person over you, but the entire opposing team and all their strategies designed to exploit and beat you.

The Calm Before the Storm

I couldn't wait any longer; I was going to pop. How could all these great players around me look so calm? Where was all the madness? All the yelling and screaming and pre-game theatrics I had grown up knowing through high school and college? Sure, there were still a few that felt the need to run around the locker room and shout out their random *Braveheart* cries. But for the most part, our star players, the ones I looked up to the most, seemed so calm, so relaxed.

Then, as would become routine, Dan walked in to make his last-minute rounds. He wanted to make sure he said a few words to each of his men. Whether they were an All-Pro or likely to never see a snap that day, he wanted them to hear from him before all hell broke loose.

I'd grown up knowing football pre-game talks as being those intense, powerful rah rah speeches. Rallying war cries from generals looking to throw more gas on the internal fire already burning in their men. Once again, Dan was different, and it caught me off guard.

His usual intense stare was softened into almost a smile. He looked at peace, maybe even happy. I watched him make his way down the locker row saying a few quiet words to each of my mates, each chat accompanied with a hearty handshake. My game day locker was at the end of the row, last stall down the line. That's what I was given, and that's the stall I kept for the remaining 11 years of my career. I would always become Dan's last pre-game handshake, for no other reason than that's just where our equipment manager 'Kato' had decided to put me. Never the less, it ended up being a very comfortable spot to be.

Reassurance Needs No Fury

For some reason, his greeting felt like my dad wishing me luck before heading off to college or going to my first job interview. In standard Dan fashion, his conversation started with a short bout of silence. Just a stare. Not the intense stare I had come to know over the last few months during grueling workouts or on field practices. This was much softer. It calmed me instantly. This talk wasn't to add fuel to the fire; it was to reassure me that no more fuel was needed. After that brief pause, Dan finally spoke.

"Angus…lead us out there, okay?" Again, a question, seriously? Was he still asking if I was okay with doing my job? He said it so calmly, so quietly. *"I couldn't feel better about having anyone else do it. Have fun out there tonight. You've earned this. Good luck."*

Wow! It's amazing how simple phrases can lower anxiety and boost confidence. He had amazing discipline to never break eye contact with anyone when talking. He also understood the power of pitch, tone, and volume of voice. Volume may reflect confidence, which is desperately needed on the battle field, but in the pre-game world of high anxiety, calmness, slowness, and a touch of happiness is the perfect thing to balance the mood and keep things (especially my mind) from going nuts.

More Than Just a Handshake

The talk-sealing handshake was also one of genuine pride. I never gave handshakes a passing thought before Dan, now I see them for what they really are: a physical demonstration of the care you feel for the person you are engaging the shake with. You could feel Dan's emotions when he shook your hand. That sounds corny I know, but seriously, like absolutely everything else Dan did, you knew that his handshake had purpose; it had real meaning, and you felt that. Never again did I brush off my handshakes as no big deal. That act means something, and what you put into your shake says a lot about your feelings toward that person and the way you care about that interaction. Dan's handshake, again, was like a father passing on his love and support to his son. Words have power, but how you deliver them can make all the difference. What just a few moments earlier was nervous anxiety had become calm and focused with a sense of certainty and belief in the actions I was about to take. That's the power a coach can have over a young, impressionable athlete.

I felt relaxed – I felt calm – I felt focused…then we got on the field to play.

We were playing the Winnipeg Blue Bombers. Defensively, they were not a confusion team. Their defensive philosophy was basically to line their men up in pretty much the same spots play after play and rely on their players' talent to beat you. From a mental understanding and block calling point of view, this would be an easy game to enter my career with. From a personal physical test standard, though, this was going to require a herculean effort on my behalf — or maybe better stated, a, David versus Goliath type performance, almost literally.

Facing Goliath

Doug Brown was my opponent. Because they rarely moved their players, I was essentially assured that I would face Doug nearly every single snap of this game. Doug was a giant of a man. I mean that in the literal sense. He was 6'8" with long powerful limbs — a rare combination of extreme height AND extreme power. I'm BARELY 6'1", with extraordinarily strong but VERY SHORT limbs – a much more common, yet less effective combination. For the next nine years until Doug retired, I would be the league's David of offensive linemen to Doug's defensive Goliath.

The Season Opening Play to Remember

All of Dan's pre-game calming went straight out the window as we broke the huddle for the first real snap of the 2003 season. My adrenaline kicked into overdrive. All Dan's training camp chats regarding slowing the game down to 5 miles per hour would still be a few seasons away from becoming my reality. Right now, the lights were brighter; the noise was louder, and the speed was a blur.

The play call was 'HOG'. An old bread and butter power running play from my earlier years. We would pull the backside guard and have him lead block in front of the running back. Nice concept, really — get a 300+ lb. man running out in front of your guy with the ball acting as a human bulldozer to anybody in the way. For the rest of us, 'HOG' was just like all the counter run plays we had in our arsenal. If our 'HOG' pulling lineman was opening up and leading the running back around the right, we all down blocked the man to our left and looked to drive him away from the play. Pretty easy blocks in concept because you have angles and leverage working for you.

It can be a little trickier in Canadian ball, though, as we have that one-yard neutral zone between us and the defender. That gives a smart defensive lineman an extra second to read what's going on and sometimes react before contact is even made. In U.S. ball, a down block is usually an act of pure explosion. You open your hip to the angle and simple cave in the man to your inside. The yard separation in Canadian ball can make blindly firing out trickier. If you are playing a savvy defensive lineman who has a tendency to be more of a 'reader' as opposed to a pure penetrator, you can find yourself "flying out the window" as Dan would say and literally missing the person completely because you committed everything you had to someone who didn't end up being where you fired yourself out to. You need a little more body control and a touch more patience with that space to make sure your defender is doing what you expect him to do before you commit to full maximum explosive contact. Film study helps.

Doug was indeed one of those savvy types. Relentless film prep with Dan had assured me that his tendency was to "read" the block and adjust accordingly. Truth be told though; my film study was the last thing on my mind. All I was thinking in my stance was attack, attack, attack. Dan had trained me to focus my eyes on a specific target for each play and block that was needed. Where my eyes focused, my hands and body followed. For this block, the target was always the defender's near hip. Where that went was where he was going. I got that far but waiting to see how he reacted out of his stance never crossed my mind. I was going to launch out of my stance on the "H" of HUT!

That's exactly what I did, thankfully it worked. For whatever reason, on that given play, Doug decided to penetrate hard; if he hadn't, I would have flown right "out the window." The speed out of my stance matched with both my focus on his hip and natural leverage angle enabled me to really drive Doug out of position. It was close to being a perfectly fitted block, just like the thousands I had done on the Crowther sled in the months leading up to this point. Doug finally worked his way off the block and instinctively ran to the play. I circled back, cutting him off on his chase. I got just enough in front to legally 'reverse hip' him (Dan's term for an old school cut block where you roll through the front of the defender's legs, chopping them down like a tree). Still full of energy, I bounced up and ran after the action and found a linebacker to shove just as the whistle was blowing. What a season opening play! A textbook down block, followed up with a 'knock down,' and finished with a down field block, all on one play.

A Plus and Two Green Dots. I Was In Overdrive and Loving It.

We got six yards on that run. Second and four meant time to throw the ball. Time to really see what I had. I was built for run blocking; my vertically challenged body gave me natural leverage to get under defenders. Pass blocking was a different story. Arm length becomes much more crucial there. The ability to control the other person with extended arms usually results in your ability to win the block or not. As Dan would always remind us, particularly in pass protection, *"He who makes first contact usually wins."* The ability to get your hands on the opponent before he can get his hands on you will greatly dictate your level of success for that block. Longer arms meant greater ability to reach the other person before they could reach you, giving you an anatomical advantage when it came to your chance of success.

A person's wingspan is roughly similar to his height. If you're 72 inches tall, your wingspan will probably be close to 72 inches as well. When you're 6'8" (even if your arms are a tad shorter than proportionate), chances are they're still longer than almost everyone else's if they're shorter than you. I don't know Doug's wingspan, but I'm willing to bet based on the length of his legs, it's probably longer than his height. Unfortunately for me, my upper limbs are NOT longer than my well below ideal stature. In fact, I was athletically challenged with not just short height, but extremely short length. My wingspan is a minus 4. Meaning I'm 4 inches SHORTER in wingspan than my already too short height.

In visual terms, I was built like a turtle. Great for bench pressing but not ideal for being a pass blocking machine. As Dan would consistently remind us, though, what matters is what you learn to do with what you're given. With Dan's tireless help, I found ways around my limitations. Never dominantly, but good enough.

Hear Only What You Need to Hear

2nd and 4. The play was 662 blah, blah, blah. The "blah, blah, blah…" was whatever the receiver route combinations were. It was probably something much cooler sounding like "X–RAIN–COBRA," but to me and probably every other lineman on the field, it was all just "blah, blah, blah." I have no idea what X–RAIN–COBRA means or what any of those chosen route code words mean, and luckily, I didn't need to. I needed to be able to do my own job and wasting precious RAM in my brain on info that didn't directly relate to my job was not only useless but possibly detrimental.

> **There is only so much information you can store and concentrate on at one time, so make sure your focus is on what matters.**

662. Easy peasy. What that meant was the back side of the quarterback was left. The right side protected firm and square. The left side of the line, starting with me, would zone protect our quarterback's blind side. Responsibility-wise, we each had to account for the space directly to our left. Anybody fills that space, and we stop 'em. Again, very easy…in concept, like most things in life. It's actually doing it that's the challenging part.

Doug was lined up directly in the gap to my left. Barring anything goofy, he would be my responsibility on this block. We already knew that Doug was a natural penetrator. This being a pretty obvious passing down only heightened the likelihood of him charging directly up field. He was also extremely bright. We knew once he read that we were back side zone blocking, he would turn and look to charge right through me.

I'd seen it many times on film. It could be really tough to stop a charging Goliath, especially when the only thing in between him and sacking the quarterback is a young David.

I wish I could tell you I had the presence of mind to think all that through and plan my strategy accordingly. But just like the down before, all I saw was my target (in this situation, his near chest pec), and all I thought was "attack." Adrenaline was pumping through my body at hyper-speed. My emotions were in complete control. I was ALL energy, zero strategy. Calmness? Are you crazy? This was football. Hyper-emotion is what it takes. At least that's what I always thought.

As predicted, just not by me in that moment, Doug read back side zone protection and turned to charge right over me. That can sometimes be a worst-case scenario, especially if he gets on you before you are properly set up and ready to strike. Directly through me (or any center) is the shortest distance for any defender to get to the quarterback. There is little time or space to recover if the defender's quick burst gets you before you're really ready. Fortunately for me, it was the very best thing Doug could have done. I was not mentally clear enough to have adjusted to any pass rush moves whatsoever. I was so hyped that I was just going right after him, again, on the "H" of the word "HUT."

I was so aggressive that I was actually able to beat Doug to the punch. I got my hands on him first because I basically threw my body at him. If he had done ANYTHING other than charge directly at me, Dan would have had a beautiful clinic clip of exactly what "falling out the window" really looks like. I lucked out. I stopped his charge and was able to hold the All-Pro dead on the line of scrimmage.

Excitedly Incoherent

The pass was incomplete. 2 and out is never the start you're hoping for, but I had never felt better. Two plays won on pure adrenaline. I was spinning and couldn't wait to share my excitement and victories with Dan. As is customary with probably every single football team from the high school level on, the o-line comes off the field and gathers at a predetermined meeting space to review what just happened. Throughout my entire career, our space was the furthest left end space of the sideline benches. Home or away, that was always our in-game meeting area.

I didn't even cross the sidelines. I went sprinting over to Dan and immediately started rambling about what I had just done out there. I have always been a fast talker, but I'm sure this was borderline incoherent. I was so excited, so full of energy, and feeling so great about what just happened. I just knew he would be just as fired up as I was. Certain he would not only share in my excitement but push me to keep it up. Instead, Dan just stared at me. He indulged my rambling for about three seconds with the confused / shocked type look of someone getting yelled at by a crazy man in a completely foreign language. Then, after he'd heard enough, his hands went up. Just as I had stopped Doug's pass rush in its tracks, Dan halted my runaway nonsense.

"Whoa, just slow down a second. Breathe." His speech was everything mine wasn't. It was slow, soothing, and calm. *"Let's just go over here with everyone and talk about what we're seeing out there."*

He said it with the same tempo that you might discuss a lunch menu. Where was the fire? Where was all the intensity, the yelling, the screaming I had endured during our workouts and training camp? Why was he so calm?

Guidance Based on What We Thought Happened

We huddled together at the far-left hand side of our team bench. Most of the starters sat; a few stood. I seemed to always bounce between sitting and standing, always too restless to stay in one spot. Dan came over with both his grease board and laminated pages. The pages were pictures of all the possible defensive looks Winnipeg had run recently. All the fronts we were expecting to see and had spent the week preparing for. The blank grease board was there just in case something new had come up that needed drawing.

I'm sure this was pretty much standard across football in all leagues and at all levels back then. Today's technology has changed, and real images of plays are now available instantly for sideline review. What a different world coaches live in now. In 2003, Dan had to pretty much rely purely on what we THOUGHT we saw out there (which many times did not match the reality that played out on film the following day) and what a spotter in the booth may have seen. All Dan had to work with to help us in those short sideline meetings was our perception of what was happening and our ability to communicate that clearly.

What that called for was calmness and focus – two things I clearly let go of while letting adrenaline and excitement rule my actions. If you're not careful, like I wasn't, uncontrolled excitement can easily consume you to the point that you lose your ability to think clearly and focus. When they're gone, you stop methodically playing the position. You stop thinking at all. You revert to what Dan would often call "street ball."— playing with no discipline or control whatsoever. You may get lucky a play or two as I did, but it never worked out in the end. The game, and more importantly, your opponent, will eventually make you pay for your carelessness.

> **Control your emotions. Never
> let your emotions control you.**

There's a common saying amongst the Navy Seals – **Calm is contagious.** Dan knew the excitement of a real game could take hold of a player, especially a young one. He also knew that most players end up mimicking the emotional state of their coaches. By being calm, he dialed down my craziness. I naturally returned to the state he presented to me. Just like back in the locker room, his demeanor pulled me back into the eye of the hurricane, back to where it's calm, just inside the craziness that is all around you on the field. That is where you need to be to be physically capable of producing hurricane-style destruction while remaining mentally anchored in the eye, able to see and think clearly. You have to use reason, not emotions, to choose your actions — to think your way through the game and to be in control of yourself.

I went back out after that first sideline dial down and played a solid season opener. I believe I graded out at 89%, just shy of earning a PayDay in my debut. Doug did get me a few times, as anyone would have expected. Each time it happened, I came storming off the field, huffing and puffing with this pissed off stare like I was going to really make someone pay.

Every time, Dan would calmly walk over and gently remind me to "slow down…breathe…and talk it through." And every time, it worked.

The Takeaway

Constant repetition breeds new patterns. I slowly learned to keep my dial in check during games, to control my emotional level, and to stay calm while unleashing full energy into a well thought out attack. Dan's constant calming force during the madness that is a football game eventually rubbed off on me to the point that nothing would rattle me. Football turned into a full contact chess match. Each move was the result of clear thought and well-reasoned action. It became so much more enjoyable to play a game with purpose, not JUST with passion. To come to the sidelines and have important conversations about what went right or, sometimes, really wrong. To be able to discuss and fix the issue without losing my mind over what had happened.

Having emotions drive your state, for good or bad, is never an ideal or lasting way to go about anything. It takes calmness, clarity, and control to create repeatable success. You need those three things to play a game as well as live a life by design based on reasoned choices. And, sometimes, you need a reminder of that. Dan gave me that reminder in between every single series of every single game I ever played for him. The lesson is now learned, and the calmness amongst chaos demeanor is now thankfully ingrained in me.

THE POWER OF THE PEN

"Angus, to work with you has truly been an honor."

~ **Dan**

It was 4:45 a.m., and I was wide awake. I've been an early riser since I can remember, but 4:45? That was a little extreme, even for me. The alarm was set for eight, lots of time to roll back over and get some more sleep. The problem was that wasn't going to happen. My monkey brain was on overdrive. I had to get up. I had to get moving. I had to go for a morning walk.

Week 2 Game Day and My First Road Trip as Starting Center

My roommate had no trouble sleeping. In fact, all the roommates I had over my career could sleep and slept well. I was always a bit envious of them for that. Even still, I had to be respectful of the time. I quietly gathered some clothes in the dark and made my way to the washroom, where I could close the door, turn on the light, get dressed, and head out without causing any disturbance. I was on my way to the washroom when I saw it tucked under the entrance door to our room, half exposed — a letter. My first thought was that it was the hotel express checkout bill. I remember thinking that seemed strange given we weren't leaving that day. Then, oddity turned to intrigue, when I realized it was a BC Lions envelope.

Why would I be getting a letter from the team delivered to my hotel room on game day? And why this early? Intrigue quickly shifted to panic. Was I getting released? Would they really release me on game day morning? Can they even do that? I had heard of players getting cut right after a game, but right before one? Seriously? I went from monkey brain to full blown panic attack. My first response was to hide. I don't know why, but I wanted to make sure I was safely in seclusion in order to deal with this embarrassing reality alone. I hid in our washroom. I just stood there. Closed door, light on, staring at that envelope, studying the thick orange stripe that went across the top, broken up only by the Lions logo nestled in the top left corner. I stared at my name, neatly written in the front middle in black ink. My mind was spinning so fast that the fact it just said 'ANGUS', not ANGUS REID, or even just REID as most of the team-issued documents did, never crossed my mind. All I could do was stare at it. I couldn't sit down much less move. For the first time, I knew what it must feel like when students are too scared to open their letters from their dream school to see if they got in or not. The only difference was, their anxiety was based on the very real hope of a positive outcome. I was already on the team. What other bit of information could possibly warrant a 4:30 a.m. team-issued letter? I'd been released. I was sure of it. As absolutely crazy as this sounds saying that now, it's honestly the only logical explanation my young, insecure, and now completely paranoid mind could come up with. Like a delusional person thinking that if they don't open their bills then they don't really have any, I found similar logic in thinking that if I didn't actually open the letter, then I hadn't really been cut. I just stared at it. All I could do was wonder what I was supposed to do next. Do I go to the game? Was I still on the same return flight home tomorrow with the team that just cut me? That would be really strange. Was I staying another night in this hotel with my now my ex-teammate roommate? Really crazy stuff races through your brain if you let it. I was young then. Focus and control were two things I was still learning to master.

After the longest five minutes I had ever experienced, it was time to take action. Time to face the reality I already knew was waiting for me inside that sealed confidential personalized envelope.

What I found inside became one of the most comforting and uplifting weekly rituals I would enjoy over the course of the next 11 years. It was a handwritten letter from Dan on official team letterhead. The top of the page had the date followed below by a typed quote. Under the quote was a handwritten note. Under that was a copy of our mission statement as an offensive line. The note was a personal message for me, thoughts he wanted me to know, encouragement he wanted to share.

6-28-03

"**Confidence comes from hard work. It comes from facing different situations and making putts. It comes from knowing you've worked on the right things, so when you get under the gun, you can execute what you've practiced.**"

David Duval, British Open Champion

Angus,

I want to let you know how proud I am of you. The work you have put in this off-season has been nothing short of tremendous. You are ready for this. I feel so lucky that you are out there leading us today.

Good luck,

Dan

OUR PLAN

1. TO BE A PHYSICAL OFFENSIVE LINE
2. TO HAVE A GREAT WORK ETHIC
3. TO PLAY WITH INTELLIGENCE
4. TO BE A MASTERPIECE IN PRECISION
5. TO HAVE A TEAM ATTITUDE

I was blown away. I must have reread it five times before I realized I had been hiding in the washroom for the last 10 minutes! I neatly folded it back up, carefully slid it back into the torn envelope, got dressed, and quietly snuck out of the room. I needed some fresh air.

It wasn't until I opened the hotel room door to leave that I noticed the second envelope. It was for my roommate. Dan had obviously written us all game day notes. As I gently closed the door to leave, I neatly slid his note half way back under the door. I wanted to give him the same game day heart attack opportunity moment that I had. Hey, what are friends for, right?

The Beginning of a Ritual

I exited the elevator into a silent lobby. The only other person there was the hotel clerk, who was either finishing up the night shift or starting the morning one. I never knew at 5am which one it was.

Then, enters Dan — not from the elevator, but from the hotel entrance. It was 5 a.m. He was RETURNING from his morning run. I'm not sure who was more surprised to see the other, but I'm betting it wasn't Dan. While I froze with confusion, he barked out with game day enthusiasm.

"Well, how's the world's greatest #64 doing today?" Not giving me any time to muddle together a reply, he followed up with an even more energetic, *"What a great day to play a football game, right?"*

All I had was a reactionary, *"Absolutely!"*

"You have a great morning, Angus! We'll see you at breakfast," and off he went, up the elevator and back to his room, I assume. I was so caught off guard that I completely forgot to thank him for the kind letter.

There's not much open at 5 a.m. on a Saturday in downtown Regina. Come to think of it, there's probably not much open at 5 a.m. on a Saturday in most places. Didn't matter, though. I just wanted to enjoy a nice peaceful walk in the cool morning air. I must have read that letter five more times as I sauntered the vacant streets. I saunter all streets. I feel walking is meant for sauntering. If I needed to get somewhere faster, then I would run.

I can't vividly remember most game day mornings anymore. They all seem to blend together into a similar pattern of generic hotel rooms and, unfortunately, all too often even more generic hotel banquet food. That game day back in 2003, though, is a morning I will remember clearly for the rest of my life.

It organically started what would become my road game routine for the rest of my career. Up early, read Dan's letter, and usually bump into him in the lobby on the way back from his morning run — always to be greeted with that same enthusiastic phrase, then off for a peaceful, private morning walk, to read, absorb and ponder, not just the note, but usually the very topical and always insightful accompanying quote. I loved it. I looked forward to those mornings and greatly miss them now that they are gone.

The Takeaway

Dan wrote each of us every single week. On home games, those letters would be waiting for us in our lockers upon returning after walk-through practice. Each letter was personalized with messages that were directly related to what Dan wanted each of us to know. It was his way of showing encouragement, praise, and often gratitude for the energy and work we put in each week. In sum, I received more than 200 personalized letters over the course of my career, not including the ones that would just randomly appear in my locker. Messages ranging anywhere from congratulations on a weekly team award, to something as simple as just checking in to make sure I was doing okay. I can't tell you how much those letters meant to me, I still have most of them to this day. The act of writing even a short, handwritten note has become so rare that the impact is massive. It touches you on a personal level that I believe no email, text, or public message can come close to matching. They were powerfully subtle, never discussed, yet always cherished.

ALWAYS REMEMBERING
THE BIG PICTURE

"You'll be fair in 5 years."

~ **Dan**

I sank lower and lower into my chair. I wanted desperately to hide, to simply curl up so small that people would forget I was even there. Impossible. Film always finds you. You can't hide from it. It shines a bright light on your performance. It is the great truth teller. It forces you to face the music, and sometimes that song you recorded the night before really sucks. The sad part is, you already know that. And at some point, earlier that morning your coach learned it, too. Now, you get to sit through the pain of having everyone else see this truth right beside you. Again and again and again, paused, rewound, paused, rewound, discussed, rewound. It's an awful experience, and the worst part is, you already know it's coming. You sit through play after play already knowing the next one up is going to be a discussion on how you just got your ass kicked – again. How the play failed or the quarterback got injured because you couldn't do your job. Dealing with that personally is one thing; dealing with it publicly, that takes growing another whole layer of thick tough rhino skin. Growing that type of skin takes time, and I wasn't there yet.

This film session wasn't bad — it was brutal. In my 11 years playing for Dan, this would go down as the worst performance I ever put out. We had just played the Alouettes in Montreal the night before and had the Renegades in Ottawa six days later, so we had decided to stay east for the week. This film session wasn't in the friendly confines of our positional meeting room back in Vancouver. Oh no! We had the great ballroom in the Marriott downtown Ottawa for meetings. That meant the entire offense was in the same room. Yes, we had different screens and did our best to carve out our own areas, but the reality was, I had to go through this public humiliation not just in front of my line mates, but in front of the entire offense. The fact that we won the game gave me a glimmer of hope that the overall mood of the coaching staff would probably not be as harsh. Nevertheless, this was going to be ugly, and I knew it.

Montreal's defensive game plan from the night before was painfully obvious. They lined up big Adriano Belli (The man the Lions traded away for me two years earlier) right in front of me the entire night. Then they had the rest of the defense run around like crazy and never actually get into any set position. Montreal's coach at the time was the legendary Don Mathews, a defensive wizard who showed little regard for traditional schemes and sound principle-based football. He would do whatever he thought gave his team the very best chance to win, no matter how crazy it may look to the outside observer. I guess on this night, I was the pigeon that he chose to exploit to give his defense the very best opportunity for success.

Dealing with Adriano was a real pain in the ass. He was a huge thick thug of a man. A tall 6'5" and 300 lbs. of natural body mass. Not weight room built, just who he was. He had extremely long arms and unbelievable power when utilizing them. What made it worse was his mentality. He cared less about playing technical football and much more about simply trying to beat you up. They talk about line play being its own game within the game; Adriano simply played his own game all by himself. He relished humiliating the person he was lined up over. Over the course of his career, I feel confident wagering that I, with my small frame and extremely stumpy arms, was his favorite target. As the seasons went on, I gradually learned to play him better. Dan helped me adapt techniques that helped me better deal with abilities and at least (mostly) hold my own.

That first game, though, was UGLY. When a nose guard is lined up directly over me, he will usually be a two gapper. That means he's responsible for the space to my right and my left. Their technique is to control me, read the flow of the play, and fight my pressure with pressure, never letting me remove them from being able to fill either gap. That night, they lined Adriano up directly over me and gave him no gap responsibility at all. He had one mission: obliterate me every single play, with no regards for anything else. At least, that's what he did…and it worked.

Most of the time, you can improve your performance by thinking through it. Any success in my career was a result of strategically understanding the play and the defensive philosophy and applying the best technique to match the two. But it doesn't work in a street fight. What a mess. I was rattled mentally because I was getting abused physically. I became so worried about surviving his next assault, that it became impossible for me to stay calm and make any sense of the blur that was happening behind him. My instructions to my teammates became straight guesses, or sometimes worse, complete silence. I was mentally frozen.

Impersonalizing Doesn't Always Help

As professional as I always tried to be, Dan was always more so. I now knew better than to ever lean on any excuse, and he knew better than to whip and embarrass me. He always saw the pointlessness and potential greater danger to doing so. He kept mistakes clinical, sometimes to the point of removing me completely from the conversation. Instead of, *"Angus, you just got your ass handed to you,"* which was completely true, he would say something more like, *"We would like to see the center have a better anchor here."* Nice and clinical. That works well when the corrections are here and there. When it's *"the center…. (corrective comment) …"* on nearly EVERY SINGLE play, the clinical wording becomes a little less protective, and things just become awkward.

Way Past Awkward

Almost every single play revolved around either a mental mistake made by me or a physical humiliation at my expense. I did what I could to appear stoic, to take Dan's corrective cues for just that, but it had gotten so bad that avoiding the obvious was creating more unease. This reality had to be confronted. It was time to deal with the elephant in the room.

The film was paused…and Dan covered the lens to completely remove any picture from the wall. He was setting the stage for something important and wanted to make sure all attention was focused where it mattered most.

"Angus…don't worry. I want to tell you something…and I firmly believe this. You'll be fair in about five years. Trust me on that."

Inside, I was thinking, *"What? Five years? Is this a joke? I won't be on this team in five more hours, let alone five more years."* Pro football is a day-to-day business. It doesn't wait for you to be good enough; it replaces you with someone who already is. Five years? And what the hell does FAIR mean anyway? I don't think anyone else heard the *"trust me on that"* line.

The "fair in five years" part did a few immediate things:

1. It broke the tension and got everyone laughing.

2. It addressed the reality of what we were all seeing with a statement I think was meant to be positive.

3. It gave my teammates a line that was used to playfully mock me with for the rest of my long career.

Dan pretty much stopped commenting on my play for the remainder of the tape. It would have been so repetitive as to be pointless. It was addressed, strangely yes, but addressed nonetheless.

As time passed and emotions from that day settled, I began to see the deeper genius in the message Dan was trying to convey. In his quirky way, he wanted me to know that progress, real progress takes time. It cannot be accelerated as much as you wish it could. As great as the pressure of playing a sport that doesn't give you that time is, it doesn't change the fact that that's what it takes.

> **Messages are as powerful as the
> interpretation you make of them.**

I let his statement play with my mind. I chose to hear what I think Dan wanted me to hear: *"If I'm going to be fair in five years, that means he thinks I'll still be here in five years."* That realization gave me comfort enough to lower my anxiety and shift my focus away from always worrying about getting cut to focusing on the long road of improvement. Day by day by day. One you control; the other, not so much.

> **Stay focused on what you can control
> and accept that the road is long.**

I'm still not sure if Dan loved winning more than he hated losing, but I am quite certain that what he cared for most was developing his players. Both as offensive linemen, and more importantly as people. He always put our development first. That sounds obvious at the youth and amateur level, but once you hit professional, winning is usually the only thing that matters. As you'll hear coaches say again and again after a win, *"They don't ask how; They just ask how many."*

Dan wanted to win as much as anybody but understood it was the quality of your how that made winning repeatable and consistent. Focusing on the how meant keeping our minds on improving our craft, not wasting energy panicking over an outcome that had already happened. Again, at the pro level, Dan may be unique in that regard. It's how he knows to coach. He believes in that way of doing things so much that he would remind us countless times in meetings that *"If they don't like the way I coach, they can fire me 'cuz I ain't changing!"*

Learn from where you've been, sure, but direct your attention to where you're going and what you're going to be doing next. That's what we could always control, and that's what's going to help produce performances and wins that are sustainable.

The Takeaway

I'm fortunate that I never put out a performance that merited that type of next day film session embarrassment again. I worked daily on improving. Some games were better than others. I learned to not let either distract me from where my focus needed to be. Learning and improving, always. Keep your eyes on the road in front of you. Dan's "fair in five" statement always stayed top of mind (probably because my teammates never let me forget it).

I've never asked Dan if there was any real, sound reasoning why he chose five years. Why couldn't I be fair in two? In the end, it really could have been nothing more than a comment to distract me during an emotional tailspin. The funny thing was, yes, I was an All-Star and our team's nominee for most outstanding lineman the following season in 2004, but maybe my greatest season as a pro was 2007. Exactly five years from my first season with Dan. That's not just me convincing myself of that either. I've gone back and reviewed my grades and 2007 was my finest season from a production standpoint. It really did take me five years to be fair, which I assume is something resembling good.

Ultimately, the road is long. You will have good days and some that you would sooner forget. The point is to never let either rattle you. Stay the course. It's the long game that matters; everything is just part of the bigger picture. Enjoy your momentary successes and learn from your occasional mistakes, but never let either deter you from concentrating on what matters most — what you do next. The next step is always more important than your last.

ALWAYS DEAL WITH REALITY

"Don't believe what you hear; believe what you see."

~ Dan

"Dan, what if he spins?"

"He won't," Dan barked back at me with absolute certainty.

"But what if he does?"

"Angus," he then paused for a second as he always would before going into long, usually humorous, monologues, *"we don't play those reindeer games around here."*

It was post-practice on day three of our week six game prep. Saskatchewan was the opponent for the second time that season, and we were going through our weekly routine of evaluating the pass rushers we would be facing in the next 48 hours or so.

Legendary Attention to Detail

Dan had this prep down to an exact science. He would review every single pass rush move each defender had brought that season, plus notable moves they had success with in previous years. They were then divided into categories and broken down into percentages. From there, each move was further broken down into percentages based on tendencies and other note-worthy markers. Dan could tell you about any defensive lineman's pass rushing habits throughout the entire league. He knew that an opponent would use a swim move attacking your right shoulder 88% of the time if they were lined up to your right. If they were lined up directly over you, though, that percentage might drop to say, only 5%. They might bring a certain move at a much higher percentage when they were on the left side of the field as opposed to the right, or big time give away a move by just the slightest tweak of their stance. Nothing was missed. I promise you Dan knew more about the tendencies and patterns of almost every pass rusher in our league than they knew about themselves. I know this because many players at the end of their careers asked Dan for the book he had on them, and almost all of them learned a ton about themselves that they had never known, but that he had known for years.

Werewolves and Wardaddies

Scott Shultz was the study subject at hand when I had asked my earlier question. He was their nose guard and the man I would face the most that game. Beyond the statistical breakdown, Dan also had a few broad categories he tended to lump pass rushers into. The two primo categories being werewolves and wardaddies. Werewolves were usually reserved for the very best, outside, speed type pass rushers in the league. Guys that kept offensive tackles up at night not knowing how the hell they would ever be able to kick to the spot fast enough to prevent them from blowing past them and destroying the quarterback. Wardaddies were your straight up monsters. Inside guys that treated you like their little brother and had their way with you. I would say Dan reserved the wardaddy term for maybe only one or two players a season. Even if you did everything perfectly, these guys still gave you a hell of a go. They usually had many ways of beating you and relied on both physical supremacy and extremely high football smarts. Wardaddies were always a huge pain in the ass, but also the most gratifying to get victories from. All other players got lumped into a variety of other categories, most ended up being seen as a mix of a few. Scott was viewed as a power / high energy guy. I'd probably agree with Dan on that one. He had physically overpowered me a few times in our initial meeting that season and was one of the very few players that never ever took a play off when he was out on the field. He always gave everything he had, every single play. I wanted to be fully prepared for round two. What if he did spin? How best should I play it?

"Angus, let me tell you something. I only believe what I see. I don't believe things I hear. The tape never lies. I have watched every single clip of Shultz there is and I'm telling you he won't bring a spin move because he has never brought a spin move. I can promise you that."

That was the end of that…on to the next pass rusher we went.

"We Don't Chase Reindeer"

Greatness requires us to battle perception with truth. Dan was always reminding us to deal with reality only, and in football reality, that means what you see on film. Film never lies. It cuts through all the player's media hype or even a team's and allows you to focus on what you actually see. Everything else is a waste of both time and emotions. This understanding has helped me so much in life. We are constantly bombarded with opinions and statements that can make clear decisions hard to make. Dan instilled the ability to battle perception with the truth. I do my best to think back to film study with Dan — to believe only what I see and to study what I see people do. That's the truth; that's reality. Everything else is just nonsense that may cloud or sway your judgment. Don't get caught playing other people's reindeer games.

"Just to Be Sure"

The next day was walk-through at the stadium. Short meetings to clean up any last-minute issues were followed by a brief walk-through on the field. It's usually a light-spirited day as the hard-prep work has all been done, or as Dan would always say after finishing, "*The hay is in the barn.*" Not this day, though. Dan was unusually fired up. Our meeting started with the film already on. The play was paused. It was a completely unrecognizable stadium with two teams in uniforms I had never seen before.

Dan didn't even say his standard good morning to us. He just stared at me. It was quite uncomfortable, really, but I knew that play couldn't have been pointing to an error made by me since I didn't even know what league that was. After an all too familiar Dan pause, he spoke:

"Angus, let me tell you something." It was slow, deliberate, classic Dan. I was so intrigued at where this was going, especially since I was ALMOST certain I wasn't at any fault. I was completely free to be engrossed in pure curiosity. *"I went back last night and re-watched every single pass rush Scott Schultz has ever done…just to be sure."*

Wait. What? He re-watched EVERY SINGLE pass rush move again last night? What did he mean by "has EVER done?" This season? His whole 3-year career? Is he nuts?

Then he rolled the tape. *"Watch this,"* he said.

I wasn't sure what we were supposed to be watching, so by default I locked in on the center…then I saw it. The nose guard directly over him shot out of his stance to the center's right, baiting him to step right to cover him, then immediately spun to the center's left, propelling himself past the center who was now out of position to recover. Okay, great, decent spin move. What did this have to do with us or Scott Schultz?

"Angus…" Dan extended that pause this time. We must be in for something good. *"I don't believe what I hear about people. I only believe what I see. The tape never lies. But,"* he said, *"you need to make sure you've seen EVERYTHING. We do need to prepare you for Scott's spin move. This tape proves he has it in his repertoire."*

He was excited now, almost seeming proud of himself, like he had just uncovered a murder mystery clue. This clip was taken from a regional Division II College All-Star game after Scott's senior year. How Dan found this film is a mystery still to this day. It's the fact that he dug it up and watched it that has cemented a lesson to me that will never be forgotten.

> **Don't believe what you hear about people. Believe what you see them actually do. BUT, before coming to conclusions, make sure you've seen EVERYTHING.**

We took five minutes during our brief individual period that day to give me a few quality reps on defending his spin. Yes, we were just in helmets, and, yes, it was just a day before practice, but in classic Dan form you only did things one way — the right way. He meticulously instructed my teammate on HOW he wanted him to spin. These reps had to resemble what I MIGHT face as close to reality as possible. This was not casual; this was full speed, all business. I may have gotten 5–6 solid reps in. When Dan finally felt good enough about the resemblance of the possible threat and the crispness of my response, he terminated the drill with – you guessed it – *"Bottle that one up and put a cap on it."*

We lost to the Riders the next day. I can't remember if I played well or not. What I do remember, though, is that in the late 3rd quarter Scott was lined up directly over me. As the ball was snapped, he shot out to my right. As I stepped laterally to cover, he began to spin to my left. Everything seemed to slow right down. For one of the first times in my long career I felt the 5 mph Dan was always talking about. It was so easy to slide back to my left and be in perfect shape to have Scott completely covered up post-spin. I laughed heading back to the huddle. I faced Scott at least 20 more times in my career, maybe more than any other player, but that spin move never came out again. I know it was a complete coincidence, but the lesson has stayed with me forever.

The Takeaway

People will say all kinds of things — but believe what you see them actually do. And make sure you've seen it all before coming to your conclusions. I now not only focus and prepare based on what I actually see, and less on what I hear from people, but I also focus so much more on what I actually do and much less on what I say. Actions are what matter. Keep your focus and attention there. Study actions deeply, others as well as your own. Everything else — is just nonsense reindeer games.

ON VALUING TIME

"There's only one way to kill time – work it to death!"

~ Dan

"How'd you sleep last night, Dan?" It was mid-October that first season, and Dan was really starting to look tired. He still brought all the fire and energy we had grown to expect in our meetings and on the field, but you could tell he was having to dig a little deeper now.

Of all the phrases Dan had thrown back at me throughout my entire career, this may go down as the most classic. Without even a moment's hesitation, he snapped back, *"FAST!"*

FAST? What does that even mean? Now, I had to know more. This was the first time I found myself prying even the slightest into Dan's personal life, but an answer like that begs a little more explanation.

"What time do you get up in the morning?"

"2:15!"

Wait. What?

"Out the door at 2:30."

Sorry? What? He was so good at hiding his humor, it was hard to decipher sometimes when he was joking and when he was being dead serious. This time, as I came to learn, it was the latter.

"Too much to do. No time to waste. Angus...let me tell you something" He slowed way down, paused, scrunched his face up the way he did before delivering one of his many intense, strongly held beliefs. *"There's only one way to kill time..."* LOOOONG PAUSE (purposefully held this time for dramatic effect) *"WORK IT TO DEATH."*

He said it with anger in his voice, not at me or the other guys in the room, but more at the thought of wasting time, even one second of it — apparently, even for sleep.

Finish with What Matters Most

There are countless stories of football coaches that have makeshift beds in their offices and live on delivered pizza, soda, and peanut butter, but that wasn't Dan. Nobody was ever going to out-work him, but he still had his priorities in order.

I came to learn that Dan ALWAYS got up at 2:15 a.m. – ALWAYS. What he NEVER did, though, was sleep in his office. He always got his work done, but he also always finished each night at home with his wife. Even to Dan, the most football obsessed man I have ever known, some things were more important. I have never forgotten that fact. No matter what had to get done, no matter how late he had to stay, or how early it would mean getting up the next morning, he always went home each night. He finished every day with what mattered most — that and making sure his lawn was mowed. Two priorities in Dan's life that were never compromised, ever. Other than that, time was ticking. There was work to do.

Time Is Valuable

I have never known a harder worker or seen a person more relentless at squeezing every little bit of work possible out of every second granted. Of the many pre-meeting lectures, phrases, and parables he would start our day with, the subject of time seemed always to be heavy in the rotation. He talked often on the 86,400 seconds that are granted to us every single day — how our job, as he constantly reminded us, was to *maximize every last one of those.* Everything was timed. Everything. If there were nine seconds left in a drill period, there was still time to squeeze in two more reps. Any movement between actual work that wasn't a fast hustle was simply *"burning daylight"* as Dan would cuss or leaving him *"a dollar waiting on a dime."* Wasting time was more than despised; it simply wasn't tolerated. It was laziness. It was wasteful, and in Dan's eyes, it was a mortal sin.

Dan lived by example. He was always prepared. Every single movement we would do in practice, right down to our technique work, was pre-planned to the second. He knew how many things we could get done and exactly how long it would take. Taking any more time than scripted was tardiness on our behalf and infuriatingly wasteful.

> **"That's five seconds we will never get back!"**

He had a sense of urgency that not even my hyper-urgent mother can match. His respect for time was incredible, but so was his respect for ours. He grinded absolutely everything he could out of us for the allotted practice times we had, but every second outside of that realm was ours. We could do with it as we pleased. He was not only aware of that; he was overly sensitive to it, to the point that even accidentally keeping us a mere 15 seconds over in a meeting would come with a sincere apology, followed up with asking us to remind him that he *owed us 15 of those seconds back* the next day. Time was to be respected. It's the only asset we all have the same amount of and the only one we can never acquire more of. I never gave that much thought before meeting Dan. Now, I can't stop thinking about it. He taught me to never waste any of it, no matter what I'm doing, and to make sure I'm doing it with all I have.

Full Focus and Attention

It was about more than just doing as much as possible, though. Dan truly maximized each moment. Whatever he was doing, he was doing it completely. Every time Dan spoke with you, all his attention was on you. That rang true for everything I ever saw him do. Every single task Dan undertook was granted his maximum attention. He never multitasked, ever.

Now, it would be easy to argue that Dan was extremely inefficient with lots of his time. He basically did everything manually: scouting reports, grade sheets, and pretty much everything else you can think of that a computer could handle. He handwrote everything, which is a painstakingly inefficient way to spend one's time. Nonetheless, those actions were never half-assed, never done without great attention given to every detail. Everything mattered; therefore, how you spent every single moment mattered just the same. It wasn't so much what Dan did with every second, but more the effort and concentration he gave to whatever he was doing. Time is always running out, don't waste any of it.

The Takeaway

Remember those letters I told you about? The ones Dan wrote? Every one of them had a quote on the top. Most were from athletes and had something to do with sports…except the one I received the day after my 35th birthday. With age, you start to see things a little differently. I had played 11 years up to that point, so my career was mostly behind me. There wasn't a ton of football left for me to play, so time became a much bigger deal to me — holding on to what I could, maximizing what I had left. This quote hit me hard and has stayed burned in my thoughts ever since.

9-24-11

Your Best Foot Forward

"Which sounds longer to you: 569,400 hours or 65 years? They are exactly the same length of time.

"The average man spends the first eighteen years – 157,000 hours – getting an education. That leaves him 412,000 hours from age 18–65.

"Eight hours of every day are spent sleeping. Eight hours in eating and recreation. So, there is left eight hours to work in each day.

"One third of 412,000 hours is 134,000 hours – the number of hours a man has in which to work between the age of eighteen and 65.

"Expressed in hours it doesn't seem a very long time, does it? Now I am not recommending that you tick off the hours that you worked, 134,000, 133,999, 133,998, etc.., but I do suggest that whatever you do, you do it with all that you have in you.

"If you are sleeping, sleep well. If you are playing, play well. If you are working, give the best that is in you, remembering that in the last analysis the real satisfactions in life come not from money and things, but from the realization of a job well done.

"Therein lies the difference between the journeyman worker and a real craftsman."

~ H.W. Prentis, Jr.
The Treasure Chest

THE RESPONSIBILITY
OF BEING A PRO

"I'm a coach. I'm not a cheerleader."

~ **Dan**

"Dan, would you ever go back to coaching college ball?"

I have no idea why that thought popped into my head, but it did, so I thought I'd ask. That's my mom in me. Unlike Dan, I have never mastered choosing my words carefully. I verbalize my thoughts for good and for bad. You will always know what's on my mind because it keeps coming out of my mouth.

"No sir!" He didn't even need a second to ponder the question. Dan had spent nearly 25 years in the NCAA ranks, having great success at nearly every school he coached at. I thought at least a part of him may long to return to the uniqueness that is NCAA football.

"Why not?"

"Angus...I'll tell you why. Because, I'm a coach. That's what I love to do. I want to deal with professionals. I want to come to work every day with men who want to work. Men who don't need to be motivated to do their job. Angus, I'm a coach. I'm not a cheerleader."

That last line right there changed everything about how I viewed not only professional football but adult life overall.

Then came another classic Dan pause, but now he was buying time. His response to my question had triggered him to find supporting evidence to back his philosophic statement. Never one to waste anything, especially time and words, Dan dug through the stack of papers beside him with great haste and absolute silence. It was so hard for me to match his silence; it's always been a terrifying sound for me. I held my ground, though. I didn't crack. I waited, mouth closed, figuring this was as good a time as ever to start practicing some quiet patience.

"Remember this?"

Dan had found what he was looking for. It was a single sheet of white paper, hand printed with three separate categories with varying colored Sharpie ink. I HAD seen this sheet before. We went through this together during my first off-season. It had been part of Dan's overview to me on expectations and accountability. It was his rule book really for what his job was and what my job was.

The top bracket broke down what he saw adding up to a player's football IQ, a term I've heard thrown around so much that it has kind of become a laughable phrase to me. When I first started playing football late in high school, I was told I didn't have enough knowledge of the game. When I retired from the sport, Dan told me I had one of the highest football IQs he had ever coached. Football IQ is nothing more than experience gained from consciously learning the game. It takes time and dedicated commitment, but, really, obtaining a high football IQ is available to anyone that really cares to learn football. He broke it down and defined it simply.

<u>FOOTBALL IQ</u> =

1. **STANCE**

2. **ALIGNMENT**

3. **ASSIGNMENT**

There was never any excuse for not being able to learn and master those three elements. None of them required any talent other than caring. Given these parameters, there was never any reason for anyone not to have a high football IQ if they cared enough to have one.

The next group listed Dan's duties as my coach.

<u>TEACH TECHNIQUE</u>

4. **First step**

5. **Target**

6. **Blow delivery**

7. **Finish**

8. **Lockout**

Then there was my job. It was really simple, yet without it, the best coaching in the world wouldn't make one lick of difference. My responsibility was summarized with one word.

<u>EFFORT</u>

He made the word tangible by adding two measurables to make the point very clear.

9. **Next level blocks**

10. **Cover all passes**

Next level blocks and covering all passes were the simplest ways to visually show that effort. It was measurable and seen by all. You either put in the extra effort in a play to look for more work to do or you didn't. You either kept running after the play with enthusiasm or you didn't. Those two measurables required absolutely zero talent. They just required bringing a type of energy to what you did that showed the level of passion and care you had for what you were doing.

At the very bottom of the page was a two-line summary of Dan's entire understanding, philosophy, and belief in the expected roles in the player-coach relationship. In BIG BOLD underlined print, he had:

<u>MY JOB</u> – IDENTIFY STRENGTHS + WEAKNESSES

<u>YOUR JOB</u> – BE THE BEST YOU CAN BE

The Best of All Possible Worlds

As an athlete, how could I have ever asked for a better situation. Dan would study, prepare, and teach me all I needed to know, and how I was to do it exactly. All I had to do was show up every day and give it everything I had every single time. Like most things in life, it was simple, just not always easy.

Dan expected and demanded maximum effort. He had no time or interest in having to fire us up to do what we loved. The concept itself was beyond him. He was there to teach, to coach, to push (sure), but not to get us excited to be pushed. We were adults; this was our chosen profession. You bring everything you have every single day.

It's very simple — don't expect or need someone else to get you excited to do your job and live your life. Coaches are there to instruct, guide, push, review, correct, and adjust. They are not there to cheerlead. Dan's little reminder of that has never left me. Professionals and adults should never require a cheerleader in life. As the legendary Vince Lombardi once said, *"If you're not fired with enthusiasm, you'll be fired with enthusiasm."* That enthusiasm is ALWAYS on you. Don't look for someone else to get you excited to do what you love.

Expanding on That Responsibility

The following season our position manuals had a new document added to them. It was the very first page inside the cover, before everything else, including the index. This sheet became the template for Dan's expectations and explanation of what our role was as professionals. As I have come to learn post-football, these expectations hold true for our role as adults as well.

The page listed six expectations and requirements:

A PRO
ACCOUNTABLE
ASSIGNMENT ORIENTED
FUNDAMENTALLY SOUND
COMPETES – FINISH!
MAKES PLAYS
TEAM PLAYER

Accountable: This came back to his NO EXCUSES list. Account for what you did or didn't do. There are always reasons; there are never excuses. Honestly reviewing the reasons gave you an opportunity to correct and adapt behavior to improve next time. Using and holding onto excuses prevented any growth. A true pro does not let defending their ego get in the way of dealing with reality. **Be accountable for your actions. This takes no talent.**

Assignment Oriented: Know your job and what is expected of you. Put the time in to really understanding what is required. I can't tell you how many players I played with who never committed the time needed to master their assignments. I couldn't understand that. Here were guys that truly loved what they did, and I believe really wanted to be as good as possible, but, still, some wouldn't commit the time to ingrain the knowledge of their job requirements. **Learn and master your assignments. This takes no talent.**

Fundamentally Sound: Master your fundamentals, just like mastering your assignments. This takes time. It's a never-ending process that must be an accepted way of life. There are no shortcuts here. Great athleticism can cover for some things, but sooner or later not mastering the fundamentals will bite you in the ass. Your fundamentals are the foundation on which all other physical performance will stem from. As Dan told me during that inside run period so many years ago: *"You can always fall back on your fundamentals"* – make sure what you are falling back on is strong enough to hold you up straight. **Learn and master your fundamentals. This takes no talent.**

Competes – Finish! This just reinforced the sheet he had shown me before on effort. **Compete hard every single time. Finish everything you start strong. This takes no talent.**

Makes Plays: There were two ways to look at this. One was from the pure athletic perspective. I played with guys that could make the type of highlight reel block I could only dream about. They could straight up pick 300 lb. men off the ground, drive them wherever they wanted to, and dump them when they had had enough. They had been blessed with the physical abilities to do exceptional things. They could make unbelievable blocks…and make them look easy.

I learned to see this statement from a different view point. Always be looking to do something that will help the outcome for all. It's a mindset of going beyond your standard assignment and looking to find areas to bring added value and improve your team's situation. There were countless times I had to adjust our blocking scheme on the fly to account for previously unseen defensive looks or had to come up with new hand signals mid-game to communicate an in-game adjustment in stadiums where the noise was so loud that verbal communication was useless.

Making plays, to me, meant being solution focused, looking for ways to bring more to the table to help, and going above and beyond the baseline of your job. **Always look for where you can make a play that will help. This takes no talent.**

Team Player: I think this is pretty self-explanatory. The concept is simple: care about the team first. In reality, especially at the professional level, egos and self-interest can easily take over. This might be the most challenging of all the rules on the list. Pro football is a world without guaranteed contracts. You are asked to put the team first yet be evaluated individually then retained or released weekly based on your individual performance. It's one of those great contradictions that can be very hard for some people to not only accept but to fully embrace and live.

Dan would reiterate this concept again and again, mostly in terms of our responsibility to each other on the line and then our group's collective responsibility to the team as a whole. We are all in this together. Individuals working as a single unit.

FIVE GUYS, ONE HEARTBEAT
FIVE FINGERS, ONE GLOVE

Two huge signs hung proudly on our meeting room wall. Those words were also repeated with great pride and frequency by Dan. He knew something so important to our success, yet so counterintuitive to self-preservation, had to be reiterated and praised as often as humanly possible. It got through to me. I fully bought in to the understanding and realization that I was there to help the team. The team did not exist to help me. Dan made me see that through his words but more importantly through his continuous selfless acts, always putting his players and team before himself.

Testing My Belief

Shattering my foot in late 2009 forced the organization to deal with some realities. I had always been too small, but now, I was not only getting too old, (turning 34 the next season) but had a foot that surgeons said I would never run properly on again. I have no idea when they ultimately made the decision that I wouldn't be their starter anymore, but I wasn't informed until a few weeks before training camp. Up to that point, I was training and preparing for camp like any other year, refusing to acknowledge the reality of my new brick foot that left me moving with a distinct limp. Wally called me in and gave me the news. They had decided to move our young guard, Dean Valli, into the center spot. I was fully expecting his next line to be that they were releasing me. It wasn't. I was still needed.

Because I had played every single snap the previous eight seasons, they never had an opportunity to develop anybody else. Dean would be coming in raw. Wally needed a mentor. He needed me to help Dan coach Dean. He needed me to be an extra 'center coach' to help Dean progress. He also needed insurance in case something went wrong.

My initial emotion was anger. Ego jumps in pretty quick if you're not careful. After all those years leading the line and giving them everything I had, putting me back on the bench was bad enough. But asking me to mentor my replacement was an added punch to my gut! How dare they! I thought, *"I can go start for any team in this league right now."* When emotions get in the way, you stop thinking clearly and run to defend your honor, pride, or whatever. I told Wally I needed some time. Time to vent, calm down, and think. I didn't have much, though. Camp was right around the corner.

I did the smart thing. I kept my venting private and spilled out my anger only to my family and very close friends. In the process, I got the emotions out, so I could get to a mentally calm place where I could think with some clarity and perspective.

I thought about what it meant to really be a pro. Dan's list was burned so vividly in my mind that it was easily accessible at a moment's notice. I ran through the list. I did this often in my career. It was a way for me to make sure I was doing everything I always could to make sure I was acting like a pro.

I kept coming back to **TEAM PLAYER**. I always said I bought into this, but I had never been tested like this before. What to do? Decisions can be hard if you don't have any rules, or at least rules that you are actually willing to follow. What could I do for the team? Where could I bring value? How could I help? A professional puts selfish emotions aside and does what is needed of him.

> **You can't cherry pick your principles and live them only when they're convenient.**

Decisions, Decisions.

I called Dan. I needed to see him. It was a tough meeting. Dan was like a loving father telling his son a hard truth he would rather not have to tell. I knew he didn't want this to be the way my career would end, but he had always been professional enough to never lie to me. They didn't believe I could perform at the level needed anymore. They couldn't go into a season with me as their guy with that evaluation. It wouldn't be fair to the team. It was always what was best for the team. They did need me, though, and Dan made that very clear. I understood their dilemma. They needed help with the transition and me to be their backup in case of an emergency.

Those were the facts. The decision on what I would do next was mine, as all decisions ultimately are. Wally agreed to release me if I wanted, and I would be free to seek employment anywhere else in the league right then and there.

TEAM PLAYER. That list kept running though my head. MAKE PLAYS. What could I do to help? How can I bring value to the situation? Where was I most needed? How could I best be a team player? How could I best be a PRO?

I already knew the answers. I just needed a little time to let my emotions and self-interest get out of the way, so I could act on what I knew was best. I agreed to bring what I could to help the team, to do whatever the team needed from me to best help our chances of success. To not do it begrudgingly. To not complain or be a cancer in the room. To be all in. To be a pro. A pro in all the ways Dan continuously reminded us with both his daily words and actions. Tough decisions like that are made much easier when you have rules and principles to help guide you.

They are even easier to believe in when the man who brought them to you truly lives them himself every single day.

I also let Wally and Dan know that I would be proving them wrong on their assessment. I privately made it very clear to both of them that I would win my job back. Until then, I would do all that was needed of me. I would be a Pro in every sense of Dan's definition.

It all worked out well for me in the end. Through luck or fate, I was needed back on the field as a starter. I never relinquished that spot again. Three more seasons, two more All-Stars, and another Grey Cup were proof enough to me that being a team player, and always being a pro as Dan taught us, tends to guide decisions well. **Be a team player. That takes no talent.**

The Takeaway

Being a pro takes no talent at all. It has nothing to do with your inherent level of God given physical ability. It's all in the decisions you make on how you want to go about living your life. I'm proud of how I handled that situation. I'm Proud that I didn't whine, complain, or act selfishly out of ego-driven emotion. I followed the Pro checklist Dan gave us. I did what made sense and matched that with what I wanted to be and how I wanted to live. Two seasons later, I received this opening game day note:

6-28-12

"Success is a journey not a destination."

Angus,

You're such an encouragement to me. You're a Pro's Pro in ALL you do, and I REALLY MEAN THAT.

Good Luck,

Dan

It was one of the most touching notes of my entire career. It was also the last season opening game letter I ever received. And despite that sad fact, I couldn't ask for anything more than having lived up to Dan's definition of a pro.

A PHRASE TO LIVE BY

"It's not what you look at that matters. It's what you see."

~ **Henry David Thoreau**

I was a little nervous. Not for me specifically, but for our whole group. I sat in our offensive line meeting room with the rest of my mates and watched the clock hit 9 a.m., and still no Dan. Dan was NEVER late for ANYTHING. That's not what was making me nervous, but that oddity was adding to my anxiety. We were in for a tongue-lashing. A tongue-lashing I was dreading ever since the clock hit zero roughly a day and a half ago in Regina, Saskatchewan.

We had just lost to the Riders. That was always bad enough, but having to hear about the way we performed had me dreading this meeting. We lost 28–2. In 60 minutes of football, we were only able to manage a measly two points — not even a field goal. All we could muster that day were two singles. I didn't know it at the time, but that would end up being the worst offensive performance of any team I ever played on for the remainder of my 13-year professional career. In short, it was pathetic. I had already had my share of embarrassing film moments, but this was the first full offensive embarrassment I had been a part of with this coaching staff. Our whole offense, and in particular, our offensive line, was garbage. Now, we had to face the music. I was not expecting a pretty song.

Back then, we always started the morning in positional meetings for a half hour before heading to the team meeting and address from our coach Wally. I assume it was a way for a more personal debrief and discussion before hearing the macro level assessment of where we were at and what needed to be done. I don't know if that is a better or worse way of doing things. For me, I came to enjoy hearing from the man closest to us first, before hearing the more removed, purely objective comments. Hearing from the people that cared about us directly before hearing just what our spot on the film board did in terms of worth always sat a little better with me. The first messenger of the news matters. It gave me context with the criticism or praise before pure criticism and, oh yes, sometimes praise.

At about 13 seconds after 9, Dan walked in. That was the latest he ever ended up being for anything ever again. There were two things that instantly stood out to me.

1. He wasn't in a rush. Dan was always in a rush, never wasting time, especially when HE was late. That was odd.

2. He was grinning from ear to ear. That was really odd, especially given the reality of the game we were about to review.

As usual, he didn't speak right away. He just scanned the room making eye contact with each and every one of us with that stupid grin, then he spoke. *"Men...I want to tell you something...and I believe this dearly."* And here it came, a phrase he would end up repeating somewhat frequently throughout my career to us as a group when things were going rough (and sometimes to me directly when he would catch me complaining or feeling sorry for myself).

> **"Every day is a holiday, and every meal is a banquet."**

I remember my immediate thought....*Dan's gone completely nuts! What the heck does that mean? And why is it so important to share with us with a stupid grin on his face right after the worst shellacking of my career?"*

"I want you to always remember that. We are so blessed in our lives to have the health and great fortune to do what we love to do." I came to learn when Dan wanted the floor to preach, it was best to just stay quiet and listen. This was one of those times. *"Some days things go our way; some days they don't. Don't ever fall victim to feeling sorry for yourself. We are so fortunate to have each day to do with as we please. Never forget that. Every day is a holiday, and every meal is a banquet. It is a gift to be alive. It is a privilege to be healthy enough to enjoy that gift to its fullest. Never waste that gift. Enjoy every single moment you have and all the great things you choose to do with those moments."* That was it. He ended it there...then proceeded to rip apart our performance.

Dan never went into that detailed explanation again. He didn't need to. The message was clear. Our lives are gifts given to us to enjoy. Dan never let us forget that. We screw up and fail all the time and that needs to be accounted for, corrected, and hopefully improved. Dealing with those failures and setbacks can be tough, and the reality of what you've done isn't always fun to deal with.

Football is a great sport for so many reasons, but one of the most practical benefits is its direct accountability for your actions. After every single play you have to face your teammates back in the huddle, look them in the eye, and account for what you just did or maybe didn't do. Then, you come off to the sidelines and face your teammates AND now your coaches to deal with what just happened, now with a little more time to review and account for that reality. Finally, the next day, you face it yet again; this time with the unforgiving view point of film. With time for your coach to dissect thoroughly what you did, critique and grade your work, then review and discuss it yet again with you amongst your peers. Such constant and continuous honest, and sometimes harsh, accountability is quite rare in today's world — but it's everyday life in football. The sport doesn't sugar coat the truth or look to make sure you feel good about what you did. It deals with reality, whatever that may currently be. Your reality in any given moment may be tough to confront, but you keep having to face it and deal with it until that becomes an accepted way to live. It's a great skill to learn.

More importantly, though, is the lens you look at that reality through. Your performance was what it was. How you let it dictate your overall attitude and mindset is something completely different. Make no mistake about it. Dan ripped us that meeting. It was brutal. Very few positive comments regarding our work were uttered. Why? Because the truth of the film showed that there weren't many. The truth of that game had to be dealt with. Accountability for our work needed to be faced, assessed, and corrected so to be improved.

That's life, and I would want it no other way. You need to be able to constantly deal with your present situation no matter how rough it may be. Honesty needs to be paramount.

The Takeaway

Dan never let me or any of my teammates run from our truth. It was always met head on with the intent to learn, correct, adapt, and improve. Pretending everything is great doesn't change the fact that sometimes things just aren't. That doesn't mean your demeanor and outlook on life ever needs to be. No matter how bad things get, it's important to pull back a bit and gain some perspective, so you can see the bigger picture. Life is great, and we are lucky to have this precious time to live it. Of the countless things I have been fortunate enough to learn from Dan over the years, the simple mindset of "Every day is a holiday, and every meal is a banquet" may be the most important. Life is hard, so you need to make yourself harder. Dan pushed me to limits I never thought possible and got more out of me than I ever could have dreamed. It took going through hell to get there and even then, the results didn't come out as planned. But that's okay. It's the struggle and the journey that make you who you are, not the wins and awards. Even more so, though, is the ability to always smile and laugh. To always remember the greatness of this time we get, and the good fortune we have to spend it as we choose.

WHAT REALLY MATTERS IN THE END

"TRUST. Five letter word. Easy to say. Hard to do."

~ Dan

It was the worst plane ride of my entire life. It was supposed to be a victory flight, a mid-air party, a perfect finish to a championship season. Instead, it was nightmare. Five hours of heartache, self-pity, and complete uncertainty of the future to come. We had just lost the 2004 Grey Cup game in Ottawa to the Toronto Argonauts — a game we were supposed to win. I say that knowing very well both teams go into the game with the feeling that they are supposed to win. But seriously, we blew that one. I mean, when have you ever seen a team set a championship game record for rushing yards…and lose?

We had handily beaten Toronto both times we met earlier that season. We were so stacked with talent that the league MVP announced 48 hours earlier was our BACKUP quarterback! The MVP of the entire league wasn't even our starter and didn't play a snap in that championship game. That's how loaded we were that year. It was maybe the strangest loss I had ever been a part of. It was my first taste of playing for a Grey Cup. Even so early in my career, the rarity of that opportunity was not lost on me. Was this my one shot, I wondered? Was that it? To this day, it's the hardest loss I ever endured as a pro.

Dealing with Defeat

Flights home after losses were almost always the same. Eyes down and mouths shut. Two things you could always count on. In pro football, every loss has to be accounted for with a reason. That reason comes with consequences. More often than not, that reason was a lack of performance by a player or several. Because there are no guaranteed contracts, accountability in our world can often mean losing your job, sometimes immediately. When a bad loss happens, everyone knows this. What they don't know is where the blame will land. Right after a game, all you have is how you conduct yourself from that point on until the film is reviewed and accountability is placed. What you don't ever want to do is act in a manner that gives thought that you don't care about what just happened, that it doesn't matter to you, and you're just fine going about your merry life. Right or wrong, that perception leaves an impression on the people that are judging what went wrong and who needs to stay and who needs to go. In the world of no guaranteed contracts, self-preservation is always paramount. Never give them a reason to think that a loss doesn't bother you. They need to know it hurts you as much as it hurts them. After a loss, someone always has to pay. The best way to avoid being that guy is to show defeat visibly. Make sure they see how much this hurts. Eyes down, mouth shut. Lick your wounds quietly. Minimize attention. Get home and hope you get to stay on the team to fight another battle.

No Next Week

This flight was different. We had just lost the championship game. There was no next week. In a way, we were all getting fired. Sure, coaches would still get up tomorrow, watch and grade film, finding their reasons and placing their blame. But in the end, what did it really matter? There would be six long months until training camp next year. Many here would be gone for a variety of reasons. Some would retire; some would be traded, and others simply released. The life cycle in football time is sometimes week to week, but at best it's year to year. That applies to coaches and even management. There was no reason to sell anything to anybody tonight in the hopes of getting another week; it was over. We had five hours of flying left to be the 2004 BC Lions. Players simply let themselves be themselves. This unfiltered honesty was kind of refreshing.

Because it was a charter, we had the luxury of privacy (and dressing comfortably). Like any private gathering, there was no fear of public reaction to our unfiltered emotions or coping mechanisms. In a way, it was just like a graduation party. Some people drank; some people hugged and laughed. Some cried, and others like me reverted to eyes down and mouth shut. Not because I was worried about what the coaches would say, just because that's how I've always dealt with sadness. I go inward. I naturally look to what I did wrong, why I'm to blame, and how it's over for me. Not good I know, but that's who I am.

I sat quietly beating myself up over and over again, reminding myself that I wasn't good enough. I let the team down. It's a horrible way to handle a loss, but it's where my mind goes. Of the 50 or so plays we would have run that night, all I could see were the two mistakes, that really had no bearing on the overall game, which I used as proof that I sucked.

An hour into this self-deprecating exercise I saw Dan quietly working his way down the aisle to find me. Almost all the players were in sweats or jeans, but not Dan. As always, perfectly pressed slacks, a crisp dress shirt, and a tie done up straight and proper. Professional, always. The only difference…his hands. In each was an icy cold Coors Light, his beer of choice. Why two at a time? *"Because service is always slow!"* he would always bark back with that intense yet sarcastic stare. It was classic Dan. This was a charter, though, and guys brought their own beers on. There was no need to wait for service. I thought better than to bring that point up. After all, we had just lost the Grey Cup. I think right now, two at a time for Dan had less to do with slow service and more to do with something else.

Real Talk

I remember feeling very uncomfortable with him sitting beside me. All I could think of was that he, too, was running those two missed blocks I made through his head. That he was also convinced I sucked and that I didn't have what it takes to play at this level and bring value to this team. I was preparing myself for a heart to heart on the reality of my ability, my value, and probably his thoughts on my future. That's exactly what I got. Though not exactly the message I was bracing for.

He asked permission to sit down beside me. Classic Dan, even half cut on a flight home from a championship loss he still knew the power of giving me a choice and asking if he could sit and chat. What was I going to say?

I was dreading this. I didn't want to hear what I knew he was going to say. I was already knee deep in figuring out what else I could do with my life since I was obviously not good enough to play this game at this level. I had completely succumbed to my negative emotions. My pity party was already in full swing. I didn't need Dan to throw any more logs on this already wildly burning fire. I wanted to be left alone, but Dan knew better.

He nestled in beside me and in vintage Dan fashion stared at me for what seemed to be an eternity. I never knew if he was trying to make sure he had my full attention before he spoke, or if he was trying to figure out what to say. Knowing Dan and his fanatical preparation, I would almost guarantee it was always the former.

"Angus…I want to tell you something." He spoke slowly and deliberately with long pauses and an intense eye lock that I couldn't shake even if my life depended on it. *"There are good players…and then there are great players."*

I was waiting for the *"and then there are the shitty ones."* I was so focused on my sorrow that it took me many years to really gain perspective on what he said next.

"The difference lies in two things: durability and dependability." Another long pause followed. I knew he really wanted me to digest that statement. I had no idea where he was going with this or why he needed to discuss greatness with me. I was NOT a GREAT football player. Solid, sure, but not great. I didn't possess the physical gifts to be great. I could master the system, learn the techniques, and give all I had every single snap. That's what I knew I could offer. Greatness, I always believed, was reserved for the superiorly gifted — for someone else.

Difference Makers and Trust

He started talking about players that really mattered, the ones you wanted on your team, and what they brought to the table that talent alone never could. I would usually nervously interrupt, always feeling I had to say something, but I could tell he wanted the whole floor for this. For once in my life, I just shut up and listened.

He spoke on the power of trust. The ability for a coach to trust that a player is physically and mentally durable enough to keep showing up, day in and day out, no matter what. To have complete trust in that player's dependability. To know that he will always bring his very best, every single time, again, no matter what.

He reminded me, as he'd done so many times before, that offensive line is the only position in all of sports that plays the entire game with its back to the ball. Think about that for a second. Every single aspect of what we do up front begins and ends with trust. No other position's success relies more on group cohesion, and that cohesion isn't static. It is reacting and adjusting at rapid speeds with little time for traditional communication. All you have is trust that your line mates are seeing what you're seeing and adjusting the way you expect them to. There is no time for anything else. Without that trust, there is no way a play could ever get blocked. I've always understood that, especially as a center.

Dan went on and on, dropping players names and examples. It was very deep, very philosophical. He wanted to unload his frustration from the loss into my ears through a rant detailing his view and blueprint on greatness. As I listened, what struck me most was what wasn't brought up. Never once did I hear the topic of wingspan, hand size, or even athleticism. There was no talk on any traditional measurables at all. What Dan cared most about was how his players chose to work, how they approached what they did…no matter what their inherent talent level was.

My Definition of Trust

As a player, I saw trust being built through three equally important parts:

1. Complete honesty with each other

2. Great communication

3. Building a track record of doing what you said you would do to the very best of your ability

Honesty came first. If there's no honesty with each other, then who cares about great communication. The track record is hard to build as well if you are unsure of their honesty levels.

The huddle took care of all three of these components. The first few seconds of a huddle provided an outlet for raw emotional response to what just happened. You huddle so quickly post-play that there isn't time for people to gather their thoughts and think about what they 'should' say. You tend to get real honesty...for good or for bad. You find out a lot about people in the first few seconds of a huddle, especially when things just went to shit the play before. Who complains, points fingers, or accepts responsibility? Who stays calm and becomes the voice of reason? Those five seconds reveal a ton about the people you go to war with. The outside world never sees any of that, but that's where you learn who you're really in the foxhole with.

Then it's time for great communication. The play comes in and needs to be called and completely understood by all. All the nonsense, good or bad, that everybody just unloaded needs to be dropped and dealt with later. All attention needs to be completely focused on the next play. The huddle is a tremendous exercise in communication training. You have roughly 20 seconds to make sure all 11 or 12 players completely understand what each and every one of them has to do in order for the next play to have a chance at success. Many times, this messaging is amidst 30, 40, 50 or even 80,000 screaming fans. It happens during freezing temperatures and scorching heat. Bottom line: it's never in an ideal situation, and the game clock is always ticking down. You probably get one solid shot at getting the information out. That also means everyone else has one shot at not only hearing it, but fully understanding it. That takes tremendous communication skills. Great verbal messaging — clear, concise, and usually loud, paired with laser focused listening skills. Full attention to what is being said, not just with your ears, but your eyes and, really, your full body. The success of the upcoming play depends on it.

Then you run the play with complete trust in each other that not only do you fully understand what is expected of you, but that you will actually do it to the very best of your capabilities.

Then it's back to the huddle to account for what you just did or didn't do. You build that track record with your repeated actions. Honesty, communication, and doing what you say you're going to do to the very best of your ability. That's how trust had always been built by the big guys up front. Come to think about it, that's probably how everyone builds trust. The only difference is, most people don't have the advantage of the repeated huddle environment to help facilitate and structure that bonding.

As close as Dan was with us as players, he wasn't in the huddle. Just like the rest of the world, he didn't have access to those honest reactions, nor could he feel the intensity of our focused communication in the heat of battle. All he had was an onlooker's view of the finished product. Did we show up physically and mentally? Did we do what we were supposed to do out there? Did we give it our very best? What a helpless position that must be for coaches. ALL they have is trust…from a distance. Trust with no ability to partake or help in the action that will matter so much for them. I never thought about trust through the eyes of a coach before. I didn't know how vital having it in their players really was. I naively thought that talent topped their wish list. What mattered most was your God given physical ability. If you had it, you were lucky; if you didn't, hey, that's just life.

If you had made it this far, you obviously had at least the minimal physical tools required to play. What makes the difference over time becomes your ability to keep enduring, to keep battling through while withstanding the physical, mental, and emotional stress, pressure, and damage that beats so many talented athletes down. The toll can become too much for some. The great ones endure longer. The great ones keep coming back. They keep showing up. You can trust them on that.

What also accumulates over time is your continued decision to give the very best you have every single time you play or practice. In this regard, the great ones become pillars of dependability for their teammates, but maybe more importantly for their coaching staff. Coaches know what you are capable of, and they have complete trust that you'll bring it with your maximum effort every single time. You can always depend on the great ones. They bring their best EVERY SINGLE TIME.

> **Talent is great, but if you can't trust talent to show up and do what it's supposed to do every single time, you not only can't win, you can't even do your own job.**

To Dan, that was the separator. With so much talent in pro football, what he needed most were five guys he could trust to always be there and to always do their best. Sounds so simple, really. Like most things in life, in theory it is; in reality, not so much.

"TRUST. Five letter word. Easy to say. Hard to do."

Trust can be very difficult sometimes, especially when your career depends on the performance of other people. I knew that oh so well on the field. For coaches, it's magnified a hundred-fold. Their job completely depends on trusting us to do what is expected, or they may get canned. What really must be tough is that they have no ability to help the finished product. All they can do is stand back, watch, and trust. I see now the importance of having people you can do that with. I see the greatness in it. It's a type of greatness that can't easily be measured or presented on a résumé. It's one that must be earned again and again by constantly choosing to endure and to bring your best. To be durable and dependable. To earn the trust so dearly sought after and seemingly so hard to find in this world.

Dan must have talked for an hour, and for one of the only times in my career, he didn't ask me any questions. He just talked. He wanted to get his point across. He never once mentioned anything about me, my ability, my performance, or my future. He merely spoke on greatness — what it really means — and the power of trusting.

As the plane landed and our 2004 season came to an end I was left thinking less about my physical inability and more about the power of choice. What I have is less important than what I choose to do with it. Dan's late night, half cut plane ride philosophy session left me with two distinct thoughts:

1. **Greatness = durability + dependability**

2. **Trust in those two qualities is the greatest gift a player can give to their coach**

Never again was that subject directly brought up. At least not in such a direct way. We got back to work the following season and kept "chopping wood" as Dan would say. Always working to improve.

Every year, Dan brought us new techniques, schemes, and other gems he had learned, studied, reviewed, and tailored to give us the very best chance to succeed. I kept showing up and bringing all I had. It's what I could do and now realized it's what mattered most.

I was very fortunate to play on some great teams throughout my career. We did make it back to the Grey Cup twice, winning both times in 2006 and 2011 — memories I will never forget. Magical moments that are rare, shared with people you've worked so hard with over time to create.

The Gift

A few months after my retirement in 2014, Dan took me and long-time friend and teammate Bobby Singh out for dinner. It was part of a retirement gift — a relaxing evening to share memories of a lifetime in the sport together. Not as coach and players, but as friends who went through hell at times in order to achieve things most could only dream of. It was a great night to conclude our football journey together. The second part of his gift had to wait. It was still in the making. In classic Dan form, he saw fit to bestow upon us the traditional retirement gift of an engraved pocket watch. It took my very British father to explain to me the depth of thought that went into such a gift. A pocket watch was the original retirement gift from companies to their long serving, much appreciated employees. A memento symbolizing, as my dad explained that, "now you have the time." The time to take everything I learned from my coach and to apply it to the rest of my life.

A few weeks later, a letter arrived at my house. It was an envelope from my now former employer The BC Lions. It was personally addressed to me in Dan's all too familiar handwriting. What I opened would come to be the last letter Dan would ever write me in the context of being my football coach.

The words hit me hard. Some things can instantly transport you to a different time. I felt I was right back on that charter plane in '04, flying home from Ottawa after that painful Grey Cup loss. Only this time, my perspective on the memory had changed. For the first time since that night more than 10 years earlier, Dan spoke again of his thoughts on greatness. Only this time, he didn't leave his opinion of how that related to me open for interpretation. There was no quote this time, nor a reminder of our unit's plan on how we wanted to play. Just a message.

5-28-14

Dear Angus

Just a short note to say hello, and I hope you were able to receive your watch by now. I wish I could have seen you, but I know how busy you are.

There are two things that distinguish Great players from Good players - Durability and Dependability. If you don't have those two things, you'll never achieve greatness.

You were a GREAT ONE when you played here, and in MY BOOK, you will always "Be a GREAT ONE!"

Very Truly Yours,

Dan

As I read the letter, a deep sense of happiness came over me. Not that he thought I was a great one, but that I was able to give him that trust that is so hard to earn. I'm honored I was able to give that to my coach. A good student is merely an extension of a great teacher. Whatever I was able to give to Dan was a result of what he put into me. I was able to give him what he always gave us.

I learned real durability and dependability from a man that was always there for me, that never flaked out, that kept coming back for me, and always gave me absolutely everything he had every single time. And, in hindsight, I think Dan was also telling me to do something beyond my career as it came to its close. In that same note, I've always felt he was telling me to "Be a GREAT ONE," whatever my next goal might be.

Dan is the most dependable person I have ever known outside of my immediate family. He gave me everything he had every single moment of our existence together. I had and still have absolute trust in him. It was such a comforting career completely trusting the man responsible for guiding my progress.

A Parting Thought

Please take some time to thank all the coaches who gave so unselfishly of their time to help you improve both as a performer and as a human. Thank them in whatever means seems the most appropriate, then give them the ultimate thanks. Live the lessons you have learned. Live them in everything you do, every moment of your life. I know I try to. It's not always easy, but that's what makes it so worthwhile. It doesn't take talent to always show up and to always give your best at everything you do. But for many of us, it did take someone showing us that through the way they coached, but more importantly how they lived.

Thank you, Coach.

THE MAN

Dorothy: "Are you not a great wizard?"
Oz: "Not a bit of it, my dear. I'm just a common man."

~ L. Frank Baum's The Wizard of Oz

My cell phone rang; it was area code 301. I didn't know a 301 number. I didn't even know what area it was. I usually wouldn't have answered an unknown number, let alone an unknown area code, but for some strange reason it looked familiar.

It was mid-April 2015. I had been retired from football for over a year and had moved into the business world. My transition was not as rough as I had feared. I was actually enjoying the totally new challenge — just as competitive without the annual surgeries afterward. I had adjusted well. I was happy. Football was quickly becoming a fond memory of something I used to do. Then, that phone rang.

"Hello?"

"Angus…it's Dan."

There was no other identification given. There was no other identification needed. All I needed to hear was "Angus," and I knew in that instant that it was my old coach calling. That pause, that voice. It was unmistakable. It was the voice that I heard almost daily for 11 years.

"Coach, how are you? What's going on?" It was nonsense small talk, but I really didn't know what else to say. I had met up with Dan a few times post-retirement. A lunch here and there. They were almost always set up via email or in person if I happened to run into him after a game or a practice I was visiting. A random phone call was not the norm.

"Doing great, thanks, and trust you are as well."

"Absolutely! You fired up to teach those Riders how to play ball?" Dan had recently been let go by the Lions after a 12-year run. A coaching overhaul had taken place, and he became one of the coaches that ended up feeling the reality of that change. He was quickly scooped up by Saskatchewan and would be starting up his first training camp there in about six weeks.

"That's actually why I'm calling."

For a split second I actually thought he might be calling to ask me to come out of retirement. Ego tends to hear things first; reality takes a moment or two longer to process.

"I wanted to see if you might be interested in coming out and giving me a hand? I could use the help."

What? He wanted MY help? All Dan had ever done was teach me things, now he was asking me to help him teach others. It was an invitation to be a guest coach with him for the first two weeks of training camp. I was floored. I really didn't know what to say. What an honor! What an opportunity! I had been completely removed from football since my retirement. To be asked to come help him coach not only made me feel proud that he believed in me enough to help coach these guys, but it was also an amazing chance to be a part of this great game again, even if only for 10 days or so. I didn't even ask the dates, didn't even check my work schedule, and maybe most amazingly, I didn't even consult with my wife. I just said YES right then and there. When your mentor calls for help, you just say yes.

Those 10 days were like no other I had ever spent around Dan. I was no longer a player but an assistant working alongside him. I was now behind the curtain. I was on HIS side of the fence. I got to see this wizard I had always marveled at for what he really was – a man. A regular man. Working beside him those early mornings and late nights gave me the final perspective on the truth behind his greatness. I saw Dan tired, frustrated, and flat out angry — all the things we all feel all the time. Dan was human! I just had never seen that side of him before. The magic came from his decision to never allow those emotions to detract from being the coach his players needed him to be. When the lights came on and the coaching day started, Dan was always on, always positive and fired up.

He made that choice each and every day because he knew that's what his players deserved, and that's the type of coach and person he wanted to be.

"Greatness, it turns out, is largely a matter of conscious choice and discipline."

~ Jim Collins

That guest coaching experience may have been the greatest gift Dan had ever given me. After 11 years of learning how to live by being taught how to play, I finally got to see the real secret. The one thing that matters more than all the others: the decision you make about how you want to live your life. How you choose to conduct yourself and go about your business. Everybody gets tired, frustrated, and angry…even Dan. There's no magical way to avoid being human, just choices you get to make again and again and again. They require no talent and don't come with a price tag. How you choose to live is always up to you. I not only learned that from Dan but also was fortunate enough to have firsthand access to the type of playbook that could help me choose how to live my life.

In 2002, I needed some serious help to get my football career on track. Never in my wildest dreams did I ever think that a coach would come along to not only do just that, but in the end, use this great platform of sport to teach me how to live my life.

I remain eternally grateful…

Photo by Jennifer Reid

Thank You, Coach